Ice Cream Sundays

First Edition

**Written by
Luella Thomas
&
Associates
Cloria T. Barnard
Marlene T. Little
Patricia T. Spruill
Audrey Thomas**

ISBN: 0-7596-6243-6

This book is printed on acid free paper.

1stBooks - rev. 04/12/02

Table of Contents

Preface

"Louvenia."

One peaceful Sunday morning, around 7:30 a restful sleep was suddenly interrupted by a stern and authoritative voice of my father. I answered, "Suh?" He said, "Get up! I want you to make ice cream this 'moaning'. I'll be back in a little while to take that ice cream to church. Gus (farm owner) had some new calves born 'yestiddy' and I have to go and see to them."

Fear immediately crept over me, because I had never made daddy's homemade ice cream before. Perfection was the only thing he was gonna stand for or a severe scolding or whipping was in order. "Yessuh!" I said reluctantly. Money and food were so scarce during those times and daddy did not want us to waste a dime.

He proceeded to give me his infamous recipe of fresh cow's milk full of cream and butter. First, the milk was boiled for sterilization (on a wood burner), and then sat aside to cool. Next, eggs, sugar, vanilla and a little flour were added. The mixture is strained for lumps, cooled, and then poured into the metal container of the ice cream maker. A dasher is placed inside of the freezer for blending and the metal lid cover the freezer. The ice cream freezer is placed inside the wooden bucket. An ice pick was used to break off small pieces of ice from a huge solid ice block which daddy would get from the ice plant. Layers of ice and rock salt were placed around the ice cream freezer. A handle for churning is placed on top. The handle is then turned for about 45 minutes to an hour or until the ice cream is so thick you can't turn the handle anymore.

After six hard grueling days of share cropping, being farm hands and doing family chores, Sunday morning church services for rural black southerners was the highlight of the week. It was a refuge from the ordinary, especially in the summer. It was a place where you could go and secretly tell all your inner pains and problems without judgement. Church allowed you to release tensions of segregation, poverty and just life in general. During the service, the minister would always give a message about the mess the world was in and a method of overcoming it according to God's plan. That was hope.

Moments after morning worship service were exciting! Adults talked, gossiped, and bragged about their meager belongings. Teenagers met to show off new clothes. Some came to date and some just to have fun. It was a place where parents trusted their children to go without chaperones and expected them not to get into any trouble. As with most teenagers, little did they know.

Introduction

This story is about the struggles of a black woman who was raised in a large poverty stricken family. With many obstacles in her path, it was difficult to place trust in anyone. She found a true friend through her silent cries for guidance, peace, and love. This friend was discovered at an early age through faith and perseverance. Jesus became her friend.

As a woman of little education, she reached spiritual heights that are unfounded in many females of her time. Education became the key for her children even though she was denied to walk through that particular door of success. Being a poor black woman in the south was bad enough, but to have no education was even worse. This would be her chance to prove to her father that education does make a difference.

Her scars are branded in her mind unseen by the human eye. She suffered so much in her life that most of us would have given up and withered away to dust. Her hands may feel rough from a hard abusive life society had to offer, but those hands have soothed away many tears.

Dedication

Special thanks goes to my children: Willie, Curtis, Robert, Patricia, Marlene, Audrey, and Cloria.

Love Mom

x

Chapter One

Young and Misjudged

We all lived together in a small house with a pump, an icebox, and no radio.

My mom, Agnes and dad, Jack had 7 boys and 6 girls. The three oldest were boys: Jonathan, Wendell, and Elliott. The next two oldest were girls: Ida and me, Louvenia. I was born August 1, 1927 and the fifth of thirteen children. The rest of the children were Jerome, Theola, Beatrice, Clayton, Sheila, Irvin, Clinton, and the last one, Harriet.

We lived between two white families. They did the best they could to help my family. They gave us their used clothes and other things. We would clean the yard for both families, and they paid us by giving us apples and pears. We did not have enough jars for canning the apples and pears, so mom sent us to the trash pile to look for more jars.

One day as we were walking toward the pear trees, we heard noises sounding like growling dogs. Whatever it was, it was more than one. We found out that it was not dogs. In fact, it was three bears sitting in the trees eating pears! We ran home as fast as we could to tell the family and never went back. We stayed home for the rest of the harvesting season.

I was ten years old before I started school. The people that lived down the road from us had children that went to school. Everyday we watched them go by with books in their hands. They teased us by saying, "You ragged children, come on out of there and go to school." That really hurt our feelings. Our father heard them, but he still would not let us go. Later, we started stealing to school.

My oldest brother Jonathan was sixteen when he started back. The same people that called us names were the same ones that walked with us everyday. We did not know these people very well. My God, they did nothing but cause trouble! On the way home one day, one of the bigger boys almost knocked the breath out of my younger brother. They fought like cats and dogs. Lord! We had no one to go to for help and finally we made it home. We told our oldest brothers what happened.

That night, my two oldest brothers told the younger brother, Elliott, how to get the best of the boys down the road. Jonathan and Wendell made a plan for Elliott. They told him, "When you get to the railroad tracks, whistle as loud as you can and we will be right there."

The next day as we walked from school, those boys came straight towards us again. One of the boys grabbed Elliott. When he grabbed him, Elliott whistled. My oldest brothers heard the signal, jumped across ditches, and came running out into the road. Jonathan and Wendell grabbed the big bullies, pulled their caps off, threw them to the ground, and beat them to a pulp. My brothers threatened them and told them, "If you mess with our brother and sisters again, we're going to beat your butts." They did not go by our house saying anything to us anymore.

Times were hard. It was so depressing! We had little money in the house and daddy made $5.00 a week. The boys were paid $2.50 a week. During the Mid 30's, the only jobs available to black men and boys were fieldwork. Employers paid men more money than they did boys. When it rained, they made much of nothing. Mom put the oldest girls to work by picking beans in the fields and babysitting at home. When winter came, we still had no money! The *Great Depression* was experienced by many.

As the children got older, the family moved to a house on Samson Farm for more room. So mom and dad decided to close in the loft overhead of our four-room house. Many storms came our way in that house, but they would always by-pass us. It is now September 1936. But this time, a storm was headed right in our direction. Those that had radios were able to pass on the information to neighbors. Daddy would make stops to the nearby grocery store to get the weather report from the storekeeper about the storm. He (storekeeper) said it was suppose to hit us within a few days.

It was revival time at our church. Revival was a special event for preaching, presenting candidates for baptism (*moaning bench*), feasting and celebration during the week with family and friends. Mom went to church early that evening and carried the baby with her. She also carried the three oldest boys with her while Ida and I stayed home. We did not understand then why we were left at home. Ida and I were helping daddy repair the holes in the roof. We heard the wind roaring, and all at once, it got very dark outside. He said, "I better go get your mother."

When daddy returned, the wind began to blow harder and the rain came pouring down. We were afraid of the sound of the wind and wanted the comfort of our parents. Our father insisted that we go to bed, and some of us went to sleep. But not me! I heard the wind blowing and blowing all night long! I was the only one awake, and I never heard the wind blow that hard before. Finally I fell asleep. I was awakened when my hand fell into some water. My brothers and sisters were still asleep.

As I looked around, water was coming from everywhere. It had rained so much during the night. When I stood up, the water came up to my knees. There was a loud noise. All at once, the roof of the house lifted up and fell back down. It scared me! I shouted across the room to my sister, and said, "Ida! Look, water is all over the house!" My sister screamed out to our father and told him

3

that the house was full of water. He shouted, "Go back to sleep!"

Just as soon as he said that, the roof lifted up again making a loud noise as it fell back down. He said, "Oh, my Lord!" He called out to our mom and said, "Agnes, wake up! The house is full of water! We need to get out of here. You get the children ready while I'll go to the neighbor's house to see if he would let us stay in his barn." Mom told us to grab a few things to take with us.

The neighbor let daddy use his Model-A car to pick us up from the house, but part of the bridge was washed out. Daddy parked the car on the opposite side of the bridge and walked back to meet us. We had to cross the bridge on foot by jumping over missing planks. We only had time to make one trip. He had to fit eight children and a few belongings in the car. Three of the oldest boys rode on the outside step of the car, four of us sat in the rumpus seat, and mom was holding the baby. It seemed like the ride took forever. Although the children were crying, mom and dad had very little to say. Mom's attempts to console the young children were lost in the chaos. When we reached the neighbor's house, he told daddy that it was too dangerous for us to stay in the barn, because his dogs were *run mad* (rabid). The neighbor drove us out to the highway and we had to walk the rest of the way to safety, because we couldn't go any further with the car. Daddy knew of an empty dilapidated house that his boss man used for storing hay at one time. And that was our destination.

Trees had fallen, wires were down, and the wind was still blowing hard. I was scared trying to step across all those fallen trees and wires. At one point, I fell between two trees. With one hand, my brother, Jonathan scooped me up and carried me on his back. Struggling against the wind and rain beating down on our faces, we finally reached the house. The moment we opened the door, the dark house had an old musty smell. It had one sofa, two broken down kitchen chairs and table, one oil-lamp, and one raggedy bed. We cautiously went inside anyway as wet as we could be, but it was good to be alive.

We were so tired and exhausted from battling with the storm. All we wanted to do is sleep. Mom made the bed for herself, daddy, and the two babies. The six oldest children sat on a sofa held up by bricks. When the sofa fell off the bricks, the children continued to sit on the chair because there was nowhere else to sit. The babies started crying. When daddy lit the oil-lamp, the babies' bodies were covered with chiggers. Some of the chiggers were full of blood. He noticed that the chiggers were coming from behind the wallpaper and he pulled it off the wall. Then, he pulled the bed from the wall and mom washed the babies with cool water to calm them so we all could get some sleep.

Three days later, the storm was over and the roads were cleared of fallen trees so we could go back to the place we called home. The water had receded. My dad and brothers repaired the bridge, cleaned up around the yard, and put a roof on the house. It looked like it was sitting on blocks sideways, but we stayed there until we could find a better place to live.

My brother and I were playing hopscotch, our favorite childhood game. I was about ten and he was eight. We were having a good time. Every time mom got ready to cook, her most untimely beck and calls would make me very angry. She would always tell me to come inside to babysit. She kept a rocking chair in the kitchen so she could keep an eye on the baby and me. But, my brother did not want to stop playing. He should have known the family's routine.

I was holding the baby in my arms. My brother asked, "Wenia, when are you coming out to play?" I said, "I have to take care of the baby." He said, "I've got an ice pick, and I'm going to stick it in you if you don't come out and play." I said, "I'm going to tell mom on you." Just then, he reached through the chair rungs and stuck me with the ice pick. As I screamed, my mother said, "Oh, my God! What is wrong with you?" Mom looked at me. She did not see my brother behind me. But when she saw the blood, she screamed at my brother! She told him that his father was going to kill him.

As if that wasn't enough, another day he said, "Wenia, if you don't come out, I'm going to cut you with this razor blade." Before I could tell my mother, he cut me! I cried again. My mother raised her hand up to hit me, but when she did, she saw the blood. She cried out loud! I dropped the baby on the floor as I stood up wiping the blood that flowed down my neck onto my shirt and on the baby. Now the baby was crying and I picked up the baby. She went outside, got a whip and whipped that boy until he could barely breathe.

When my father walked through the door and wanted to know what was going on, mom told him everything. He saw the blood on my neck, clothes, and the baby. He told Jerome that he was not going to leave breath in his body when he got through with him. My father whipped that boy until my mother said, "That's enough, Jack. You are going to kill the child!"

He was so sore that he could not sit for about 2 to 3 days, and he had to stand up to eat. Jerome did not ever try that again. I wondered why he would do such a thing, and why mom had the rocking chair in the kitchen?

In instances like these, I felt like a stranger in my own house. It was in 1938 when grandma Millie came to visit one day. My sister, Ida and I would often "straightened" her hair. In those days, black women used hot iron to flatten out the natural curls. She told my mother, "Agnes, I don't want Ida to straighten my hair this time. Let Luwenia do it today."

As I began to straighten grandma's hair, Ida started to examine my work. I told her, "Ida, I can do it." My mother screamed and scolded me for saying that. Grandma Millie looked at her and said, "You know, I've been listening to you yell at Louvenia all day, but you never yell at the rest of the children. She can do nothing to please you. She's liable to turn out to be the best child you have." Grandma soon went home but her statement made her think. Mom was quiet for much of the afternoon. Being so *young*, I was *misjudged* by my mom and daddy.

For years, I thought I was the problem and it was my fault. She did not love me. After my grandma's visit that day, my eyes opened and I took notice of everything around me. Things did not improve much, but at least I knew it was not all my fault. It seemed like mom wished that my oldest sister (Ida) was more like me, but she wasn't.

There was a black family living down the road from us. The two boys were actually uncle and nephew, but they were raised together as brothers. My father said that something was going to happen to those two boys, because they were inseparable and they were always into mischief. They walked up and down the road all day. When you saw one, you saw the other. In passing one day, they stared at my father. My father asked them, "Why are you walking back and forth so much with your uncle? Is someone sick? Is there something wrong?" They said, "Ain't nothin' wrong. We do everything together. We sleep together, we eat together, we walk together, and we are going to *die* together."

One day, a terrible thunderstorm left dangling electrical wires and broken down trees in the road. One of the boys saw the live wire and said, "I'll touch it if you will touch it." The boy touched the wires, but he could not let go. When the other tried to pull him away, they both died together just like they said. A short while later, a "dead wagon" came by our house carrying the two bodies. My family moved in a house on the highway after that incident. I felt like I had moved in town. That was when I saw a little change in the way we lived.

I was 12 when mom was sitting around the table with all her children. She said that my oldest 3 brothers had been to the *moaning bench* (as we called it in those days). Ida and I were told that we had to go, too. We looked at each other with curiosity. We asked, "What was that?" Mom said that it is for you to know what good or bad is" before you get baptized. If you live righteously, you will go to heaven. But, if you live a sinful life, you will go to a place to burn forever." I started to cry. I didn't want to burn forever. Now, I understand why mom took the boys to church that evening before the big storm." They were going to the *moaning bench.*

Soon after that talk, it was revival time at church again. It was a cool September night. I got dressed and walked to church, crying all the way. By the time I got there, my shoes were dusty. I pulled up a little bit of grass to wipe off my shoes. When I got inside, they were singing. All of the moaners were sitting on this long bench on the front row. They stared at me as I came in crying. There were a lot of children my age already sitting on the bench. They looked at me and wanted to know why I was crying.

I did not know anything about Jesus, because daddy didn't allow anyone to talk about Jesus in the house. I became curious about this person after that night and wanted to know more. I began to read the Bible and a little book given to me by the Bible Youth Program Union. It wasn't long before I found out. For instances, I got to know Him when bad things came my way; there was something inside of me saying, "*Don't do that.*" If you want to be right, then you have to listen to the voice of God.

Things began to happen to me that I did not quite understand or could explain. For example, mom wore a ring on her right hand. She got angry with me because Ida and I were having a teenage quarrel, and mom overheard the argument. At one point, I told Ida that I was going to tell daddy on her. The mere fact that "I" made that statement infuriated her. She called the two of us into the kitchen and asked me, "You're going to do what?" She took her right hand and raked that ring down my face. She whispered to me, "If you tell your father about this, I am going to spank you." When daddy came home, he immediately saw the mark. Interestedly he asked, "What is that mark doing on your face?" I did not say a word. My father asked the same question again. Mom gave me a threatening stare.

Then, my father asked my mother, "Are you covering up something? Did you do this?" Sheepishly, she bowed her head. "If you do this again, I want you to take your clothes and go back to where you came from," he said. I could not understand my mom, and why would she intentionally inflict bodily harm to her daughter. Maybe my family did not know the difference between right and wrong. My Lord, help them all.

My brother, one of my little sister, Theola, and I had been to school. On our way back, my grandfather called us to him. He yelled, "Come here!" We walked over to him. Then he asked, "What did you learn in school today? Do you know how to spell cat?" My little sister said, "Yes." My grandfather said, "Let me hear you spell cat." Theola spelled it, c-a-t. My grandfather said, "No. That is not how you spell cat. This is the way you spell cat, b-a-t. That is the way you spell cat." After he spelled cat, he clapped his hands loudly, threw his head back, and let out a loud laugh, grinning from ear to ear.

He had a hammer in his hand and was fixing the gate. We noticed the horses in the gate. As soon as we got further down the road, the four horses broke down the gate and came galloping behind us. We ran for about a mile trying to reach the edge of the woods across the road from our house. Before we could get to the woods, we had to cross over into a field of peas.

My sisters (Ida and Theola), and I hid from the horses by lying down in the pea field. The horses were so close that they were breathing on us, but we did not move a muscle. If they had taken one more step, they would have stomped us. Then the horses turned and went back the other way. When they turned and ran back, we got up and ran towards home. They got to the highway and turned right back and came toward us again.

By the time we reached the front porch, the horses were there in the yard, too! My mother asked, "Where is your brother?" She did not know that the horses chased us home. It was dark when my brother Jerome came home. We found out that he had climbed up a tree but dropped his notebook and books on the ground. He was so upset, because the horses stomped and destroyed his papers. If my grandfather had not been laughing and clapping his hands, the horses would not have broken down the gate. My father told us not to go to our grandfather's house again.

Turning every idea into a profit, my father went into business of cleaning chitterlings. In the backyard, there was a big ditch that the prisoners dug. The rushing water in the ditch was always looked clear enough to drink. We put on our aprons to clean the tubs of chitterlings my father brought back home. We cut pieces of chitterlings, put them in the rushing water, and the chitterlings were cleaned. After they were cleaned, we made a fire to cook them. Daddy sold them in dishpans.

We cleaned about 6 tubs of chitterlings a day. At the end of the day, the stench of chitterlings was foul, but we continued to clean them each and every day. We never received any money for the work that we did.

Unexpectedly, my father came home with a new car. My mother asked, "Are you going to give us some of the money? We work hard, too!" He said, "Well, the next time I'll give you all some." He had the look as if he had never seen us before. Mom said, "I'm sorry! There won't be a next time!" I was so glad she said that. I got tired of cleaning chitterlings, anyway!

We grew up working hard. It seemed like we were getting nowhere, but we kept at it. Daddy, Jonathan, and Wendell worked on the farm. Elliott joined the Army to fight (World War II). Ida and I started washing clothes for people. Ida was 13 and I was 12. We were paid fifty cents for each washing. Sometimes we washed for two families per day, and we were paid one dollar. We washed everyday for different families. By the end of the week, we made five dollars. We continued to wash clothes until I was 14.

To make ends meet, daddy had an idea to make homemade ice cream to sell at the church. The recipe was passed down from his mother from generation to generation. For this idea to work, he needed the help of all the children to take turns making the delicious *ice cream*. He needed a place to sell it, and he chose to use mom's portion of the family land beside the church, which he had paid taxes. He felt that he had the right to use the land. The family gave him the privilege to use it and he built an ice cream shack.

He said to mom, "If it was good enough for me, it was good to sell." He did not realize that one gallon of ice cream could go so fast. The next time he sold ice cream, he made two gallons. My father sold *"Ice Cream"* on meeting *"Sundays"*. After three years, he decided to buy a larger freezer. This time the freezer was 2 ½ gallons, and altogether, he had three freezers, which made a total of 5 ½ gallons.

11

"Luwenia." One peaceful Sunday morning around 7:30, a restful sleep was suddenly interrupted by a stern and authoritative voice of my father. I answered, "Suh?" He said, "Get up! I want you to make the ice cream this 'moaning'. I'll be back in a little while to take that ice cream to church. Gus (farm owner) had some new calves born 'yestiddy' and I have to go see to them.

Fear immediately crept over me, because I had never made daddy's homemade ice cream before. Perfection was the only thing he was gonna stand for or a severe scolding or whipping was in order. "Yessuh!" I answered reluctantly. Money and food were so scarce during those times and daddy did not want us to waste a dime. I worked hard before he returned from feeding the cows. It was only minutes after everything was done when daddy drove in the yard. He went inside and came out towards me with a spoon. He lifted the lid and tasted the ice cream. The suspense was killing me! He turned and smiled in approval of a job well done. Since I had worked so hard, I knew that I would receive a small reward, not even one small bowl. The ice cream was taken immediately to the church, and I knew then that I had inherited another chore.

Chapter Two

Falsely Accused

Since United States was at war in 1942, we worked even harder. It was scary in war times. We had to do all our work during the day. At night, we were told not to have any lights on in the house. Everyday I continued my routine of washing clothes for pay and running home soon as the chores were done. My parents kept close tabs on all the children.

The war made it hard for everyone; the men fighting and the families they left behind. We could not understand why everything was so scarce because we were so young. Often times, distant relatives and peers laughed at my clothes and living conditions. But, I knew that I was blessed with a gift to sing and I loved going to church. The church became my refuge. One evening as my father was taking me to church, he turned and asked me, "How long are you going to be out here?" "Just as soon as the church turns out," I said. He said, "I'll be back by then." I was 14 years old singing in a church choir.

When we finished singing, I looked outside and daddy was not there. It was getting dark and everybody was leaving the church. There was a dirt road in front of the church, which led to the main highway to my house. Rather than wait at the church alone, I started walking towards the main highway in hopes of meeting my father. Pulling my new red coat together for warmth as I walked, scary thoughts of young girls being molested by men in situation like these ran through my mind.

Just a short distance from the church, I heard a loud noise. It sounded like someone stepped on a dry limb in the woods. I stood very still in the middle of the road for a moment listening for another sound. Unsure of who or what was in the woods, I started running. Thinking that some children were trying to play Halloween tricks, my elderly cousin came outside running with a sheet over her head. She had no idea what was actually happening at that moment!

Back then, the road plow would plow the dirt in the middle of the road. Whenever it rained, the water ran off the road making the surface hard and even. I got in the middle of the road for better traction. I could really run, but I did not like running for my life. Whatever was behind me could not keep up. I ran so much until I was almost out of breath.

Reaching my aunt's backyard, I felt someone hand grabbing my belt on my coat. He pulled on the belt and broke it. I got a quick glimpse at this man earlier. I remembered seeing him at church. He came so close to me that I could hear him breathing. Suddenly that face was familiar. It was Terry! I struck him on the side of his face. Before I could think of what to do next, he hit me so hard that I almost fell to the ground. Refusing to give up, I started to run even harder. This helped me to get away from the young man, so he whistled for backup.

I kept right on running through a shortcut off the dirt road and across the fence into my aunt's backyard. Just as I ran through her yard, daddy drove up in the driveway. My aunt said, "Who's that? Louvenia was that you running through the yard?" I said nothing. Just then the two young men jumped across the fence and said, "Where in the hell did she go?" I heard my aunt say, "Who are you? What are you doing in my yard?" They said, "There she goes, man. We better get out of here. She's getting in the car with her father. We're going to be in trouble if he sees us."

When I got in the car, daddy told me that he went to church looking for me, but I was not there. Daddy asked me what happened at church. I told him what happened and he drove me home. Once inside, daddy called to mom, "Agnes, see to Louvenia." Mom said, "Oh my Lord! What's wrong?" Daddy said, "She was attacked by Terry," quietly heading out the door with his gun. Mom said, "She has been out there acting fresh, now!" When daddy heard mom say that, he came back in and said, "Louvenia, come go with me."

We drove over to Terry's house. His father came to the door. He said, "Jack, why are you in my yard with a gun?" My father told him the whole story. Terry's father said, "You are not the only one with a gun." My father said, "I know that, but you have to go get yours. I got mine in my hands. If your son ever hurt my daughter again, I'll kill him for sure." I did not see Terry for a long time. Mom was wrong about what happened that night.

My sister was 15 and I was 14 when we went our separate ways. She worked for a family that paid her $5.00 a week. Mom took in washing for awhile, but she soon had to stop. She had so much to do for her own family that she could not keep up. When everybody came home from work, we would be so tired we could hardly talk. We wanted to save our strength for the next day.

I was serving tables for white families by the age of 14½. Ida was not the only one who knew how to make a living. The family moved from place to place. In some of the places, we barely had enough food to eat, but we kept going. It was getting close to the end of the week. It was a good feeling on payday, but we gave all the money to mom.

One day, the owner of our house was pouring out some sweet potatoes and whole ears of corn. Jerome and I went over and asked the man if we could have some sweet potatoes. He said, "Yes, but don't come back." Things really went downhill for us.

It was time for us to go back to school. Here it goes again. Daddy would not let us go to school. We would get dress for school, then, daddy would say, "Get those clothes off. You are not going to school today." He wanted Ida and me go to the backside of the field and set out some plants. He would ride by to check to see if we were still working in the fields. Just as he went by, I ran to school. I knew that I did not smell clean, but I was learning. Learning how to read made me feel good. That was all I wanted to do. I did not care about how I looked. I kept doing that every chance I got.

Everyday he would say the same thing, "You are not going to school today. You are going to help me in the field." All we could do was cry, but it didn't change anything. I made up my mind that I was going to make it. I saw that he was not going to let us go to school. It had happened so many times before. I decided that I was going to learn somewhere. Since he forced me to quit school in the fifth grade, Sunday school was the place to be. The Sunday school teachers saw to it that we got what we needed before leaving class. That is how I got to know all the things I wanted to know. I learned a lot about God, how to spell, and how to get along with people. I learned also about what was good and what was bad.

At the age of fifteen, I was serving tables again. I can't tell you that it wasn't work, because it was very hard. I learned a great deal about how to cook. I cooked beef roast and gravy, chicken pot pie, and some of the hardest things to cook for a 15 year-old girl. Cooking homemade cornbread and biscuits were difficult tasks, but I was not afraid because I asked Jesus to help me.

The lady's husband that I worked for told me to go to his sister-in-law's house for some potatoes. I finished cooking for the night. I wondered why he wanted me to go get more potatoes. Out of obedience, I went anyway. It was almost time for me to go home. The lady said,

"Louvenia, leave the food right where it is. Turn the stove on low and go home. Set the table before you leave." I cooked and cleaned the house all day. She had a lot of people coming over for supper that night.

Everything was going very well. My aunt was working over to the house where I had to pick up the potatoes, right across the yard. There were female college boarders in the house at the time, and I walked across the yard to pick up the potatoes. After leaving his sister-in-law's house, I returned to the house to tell him that there were no more potatoes left, and I went home.

It was a Friday night and that meant a day off on Saturday; I was glad. Early Saturday morning, mom told me to take some dinner to my brothers. I took off on my brother's bike. When I got to the field, they were gone. Before I could get back in the yard, some policemen came up to me and said, "Get in!" My father always told us not to get into peoples' cars and that was what I told them. That made them mad. I was riding my brother's bicycle at the time. But when I did not get in, he came around the bicycle, threw the bike in the ditch, opened the car door, and forced me into the car. As he pushed me into the car, he slapped me hard three times and called me a *black son of a bitch*.

I thought to myself, what in the name of God had I done? The three policemen drove me out of town. We went up a dirt road and all of them got out of the car. One punched me on one side and one punched on the other. One policeman pulled off his belt and beat me on the head with the belt buckle. Before I fainted, I asked myself what had I done to receive such punishment. They had beaten me unconsciously to the ground. When I woke up, I did not know where I was.

The policemen made me say that I had given the money to my father, and that's why he was jailed for 30 days. He was so brutally beatened that he could not move his hands. His fingernails were black because the fingers had swollen double in size. My father asked me, "Louvenia, why did you tell them that you gave the money to me?" When I was about to tell what really happened, the policemen would not let me talk. They said that if I ever told on them, they were going to kill me the next time. Those men could take me out anytime they wanted.

They were going to arrest my brother Wendell too. But my father's boss (Gus) said, "If you don't let these people go, you are all going to be in trouble." These people had been working around me for many years, and I never had any problems. Now, let these people out of here. I need these people to go back to work."

My brother was driving the log truck, so they let Wendell go and then my father. As for me, I had to stay in the rest home for 30 days. They could not put me in jail because of my age, so they put me in a rest home. This rest home was filled with mental patients and people who could not live alone. It was a sad place to be. Out of all the days that I stayed in the rest home, not one family member came to visit me. I had nothing or nobody, not even a change of clothing. Being a fifteen-year old, I did not have anything clean to change into when it came that time of the month. I felt helpless.

Soon it was time for the trial. The owner of the rest home came to me and asked, "What are you in here for?" Then, he looked me straight in the eye and said, "Let me look at you. Look me straight in the eye. I'll know if you took that money or not. Did you get that money?" I said, "No, I did not." As I looked at that man, tears began to roll down my face. He took his hand and wiped away my tears. He said, "You did not get that money. I can look at you and tell. If you did not get the money, say so, and stick to it."

Then, he asked, "How old are you?" I said, "Fifteen." The owner of the rest home knew the man and wife who had me arrested. He told me that those people had set me up. I thanked God that I had found one person that believed my story.

In the morning, I was told that my trial was later that same day. My lawyer did manage to get me a change of clothes. It felt so good to have some clean clothes.

The lawyer and a car were waiting for me outside. As I got in the car, my lawyer greeted me with a good morning and I returned a good morning to him. The owner of the rest home waved to me good-bye as I was leaving. My lawyer told me that I was going home that day.

As we walked into the courthouse, I noticed that it was full of people waiting to see me in court. This was one of my worst days in my life. All eyes were on me with each step. I kept walking and one policeman threatened me and whispered, "You know what I told you." The mean policeman told me that again when I was called to the stand. Gus was in the audience looking directly into my eyes.

Then the judge asked me to raise my right hand and said, "Do you swear to tell the truth and nothing but the truth so help you God?" I said, "I do." The judge asked me where I worked? I told him. The Judge's next question was, "Did you go over to the next door to get anything?" I said, "Yes." "What did they tell you to get?" I said, "Potatoes." "While you were there, did you see a billfold?" I said, "No." They pulled out 5 billfolds and asked me which one did I get the money out of? I said, "Neither one. I have not seen the billfolds before."

The lawyer representing me yelled out, "Let her go. She did not get the money." They kept telling me that I knew where the money was. My lawyer said, "If you don't let her go, you will be in a mess because I am going to sue all of you." That is when they said, "Let her go home."

When I got home, Mr. Gus was waiting in the yard. He told daddy to sue the people for causing us so much grief.

Daddy saw what looked like a white spirit go under the porch. In those days, old folk believed that seeing guardian angels dressed in white was a sign of death. Daddy said, "No." He was not going to press charges because of what he saw. But, that night, Irvin died at the age of seven. He had internal bleeding caused by worms. He did not stay with us long. It hurt so much to know that I would never see my brother again. After the funeral, we all grieved for days.

It was not the same. My brothers and sisters were looking at me as if I was a stranger in my own home. I had done nothing wrong nor did I steal the money. They made me feel like a criminal. It seemed as if they believed everything the policemen said about me. I could tell that they all had doubts. I was going to hold up my head and keep going. It was hard but I kept on trying.

When this happened to me and losing Irvin at the same time my father almost lost his mind. Everything changed around our house. After the incident, people would see me and ask, "Are you the one that was in that mess?" I felt really bad when someone would see me or ask questions about the incident. The thoughts even haunted me during the night in bed. I convinced myself that I did not do anything wrong. I told the Lord that I did not do anything wrong. By talking to the Lord, it made me feel better.

After court and everything was over, the people that put me through all of that turmoil wanted me to come back to work. No way! I will not go back to work for those people anymore. I thank my God I'm still alive!

Mom knew daddy did not want me to work for that family again. She needed the money for herself and the other children. The lady came to our house begging my mom to let me work for them again. The only thing that mom saw was the money. I told her I did not want to go and began to cry. She just said, "Just go ahead and get dressed."

Daddy happened to come home about the same time as the lady came into the yard. She said, "Can I speak to Louvenia?" My father said, "For what?" You are the lady that caused my daughter all of this ruckus. Now, you want her to come back to put her into more trouble? Get out of this yard, right now and don't you ever come back!"

During the trial, the lady caught her husband in a lie. Praise the Lord! Finally, the truth was out in the open. I later found out that the lady's husband had given one of the college girls some money. He had given her $500, and they "accused" me of taking the money. She left him after that. Then, he had a heart attack and died. My lawyer later told my father to sue the people who had me arrested, because I had been *falsely accused* of a crime I did not commit. Daddy said no. He did not want anymore trouble. No one can hurt one of God's children and get away with it.

One thing my father always told his children. We were to keep our hands off other peoples' things. If we didn't, he would give us a killing (beating, spanking, etc.). We knew he would do just that.

Chapter Three

Last Wave Good-bye

Well, I did not go back working in houses after that. I went back to the field: picking beans, potatoes, and cutting cabbage. Daddy showed me how to pick beans (snap beans). In one-half day, I picked 27 crates of beans. Everything I did came out a winner. I had no doubt in my mind that things were not going to work.

It was not long before brother Jerome, my younger sister Theola, and I went to Providence (NC) on a truck to pick beans. By the time we got to Providence, people were already picking beans. I loved to pick beans after I learned how to do it well. Each day I would pick at least 25 crates. The owner would say, "Where is my girl that picked so many beans?" I turned around and looked at everybody to see if they were going to raise their hands. They didn't, so he called my name. Proudly, I held up my hand. We picked beans until the season was over.

Then, we cut cabbage until December. Later that year, oldest brother Jonathan got married. It was not long before the next oldest brother Wendell got married, too. Elliott was still in service. We had not seen or heard from him in a long time. The family was anxiously waiting to hear from him. When we did hear some news, the authorities told us that the ship he was on had broken in two pieces. They could not find Elliott and his shipmates, but they were searching for the wreckage.

When my brother finally returned home from serving time during World War II, he told us of the story of how the ship split into two pieces while facing a raging storm. The ship began to rock. He was talking with some of friends when the ship broke apart. He sadly watched some of his friends being attacked by vicious sharks. He, along with the other survivors, was shipwrecked for 18 days. The Lord just blessed him to come home safely and unharmed.

As my brother settled down at home, he went to school. His trade was carpentry. He could make anything you wanted. He made wardrobes, cabinets, lockers, and so many other things. You name it; he could make it. Well, that was a head start for him. He stopped and went into millwork. He stayed there for a very long time.

During our teenage years, Ida and I would go to church alone. Ida was 17 and I was now 16. We had become kind of close now having to defend ourselves from our neighborhoods and church rivals. We would watch the boys more since we were teenagers.

The first time my older sister introduced me to two brothers. She had one and I had the other. They took us for a ride in the car. That night, things did not go so well. The young men wanted more than we had planned. We scuffled and wrestled that night. My date called me a wild animal and everything, but he didn't have his way with me.

The second meeting with two different boys was much better. Ida picked her a tall guy from another part of town who could dress really well. She told me that her boyfriend had a guy for me. I was in church at the time. Ida came in church and whispered, "Your boyfriend is outside." I said, "What boyfriend?" She said, "Come and see." He told someone to tell me to come outside. I did not want to leave before the church service was over. Curiously I whispered, "How does he look?" She said, "Come on and find out for yourself!" Slowly we walked nervously to the front door.

As I was standing at the front door, there was a guy at the bottom step looking up at me. I gradually moved to the church steps when he said, "Come on down."

When I approached him, he said, "Let's go for a walk down the road." We learned a lot about each other in the few moments that we shared. We exchanged names, goals, and desires. As we talked, I did not lose focus on the fact that we (my sister and I) must be home before the sun went down. That evening, Ida and I promised to keep this secret between us. For the rest of the week, I was bubbling all over! I had nothing on my mind but going back to church in hopes of seeing *him* one more time.

This secret lasted for about a year. By that time, I was 17 and he was 21. My father did not know about this secret relationship. My friend's name was Jared. He had qualities that no other young man in my small town had. He had a job, owned a car, dressed really well, and wanted to be married. To me! And most of all, he wanted me to go back to school and get my education. So he decided to take me home one day. This made me very nervous knowing how furious daddy would be. It felt like my heart was in my throat. Ida and her boyfriend were in the back seat. As we drove into the driveway, daddy was on the porch. My God! When he recognized who was in the car, he went directly inside the house. While he was inside, we all got out of the car. Daddy came back outside with a gun in his hands. He said, "Get out of this yard before I shoot you!"

Jared turned and said, "I'm not afraid of you!" I'll..." Immediately I said, "No Jared, go home, please!" We continued to meet each other at church on Sundays, but I felt that things were not the same. I had a feeling that he was going away. Later, he told me that if he stayed, he would have to kill my father. The last Sunday we met, he said to me, "I will be leaving tomorrow at 7o'clock in the morning. Be on the porch so that I can see you before I leave." That Monday morning before 7 o'clock, I was standing on the porch when daddy saw me.

Daddy asked, "What are you standing on the porch so early in the morning?" I did not know what to say. I was silent for a moment. Then all at once, I heard a horn blowing. I knew it was Jared. I gave my *last wave goodbye* as tears ran down my face! After the car passed, my father asked another question, "Who was that?" I felt numb all over, and I still did not know what to say. Mom broke the silence by saying, "Jack, are you ready to eat?" I was glad that was over, but mom jumped all over daddy. I eavesdropped and heard her telling daddy about himself. She said, "I'll be glad when the children get grown so that they can have some freedom."

I thank God and my boyfriend for leading me down the right path. I never had a doubt in my mind; Jared was the right man for me. When he drove by the house that morning blowing his horn, he carried the old me with him and a new me had to step in to start all over again. I never saw him again.

Another family moved close by. We did not know the family but daddy later learned more about them. He found out their kinfolk and the place they came from before moving next door. My father had some old friends. One was always coming around. He came mostly on Sundays so that he could get a free meal. After we came home from church one Sunday, he told daddy that one of his friend's oldest son, Wilbert was nice. Well, what was that leading up to, I wondered? I noticed every time we looked up this man would be going by. He did not come in, because he knew how daddy was.

Every time Ida and I went to church, this man followed us all the way there. On our way back home that afternoon, he followed us home. We both agreed that this man was crazy! We ran inside to tell our parents about it. Without saying a word, daddy got up and went outside to sit on the porch. I said to myself, what was my father thinking about? He didn't even get mad about this strange man following us home.

In those days, fathers and mothers were looking out for themselves. My father's friend did a favor for him a while back. To repay the favor, my father told this man that his son could see one of his girls. I said, "Oh, my God. This man is too old for us." Looking at me, my father said angrily, "No one else is coming here to see you but him." I cried.

The next Sunday, this same guy was following us to church. He had on overalls. I asked him, "Why are you following us?" He said, "I want to talk to you, and your father said that it would be all right for me to see you." I thought about it. As long as I stayed with my parents, I could never make my own decisions. Maybe this was my chance to get away.

This man had been watching me for a long time. He watched me go to work and church. He knew that I was a working woman. I just wanted to know, why didn't he ask for my sister? My sister and I were a lot different in many ways. Everything my hands touched turned into something great. My Jesus made it work. I did not stop when things got bad. I cried, prayed and moved on.

I could tell this man did not like to work. It was a perfect sunny day and he was not working. When asked why he wasn't working, he said that he was sick. Later that summer, Wilbert asked me to marry him. Since my father said that no one else was coming to see me, I told him to give me some time to think about it.

One Sunday coming from church, Wilbert was walking Ida and I home. Ida started playing around with Wilbert. She played with him until she fell in the mud puddle. Her Sunday clothes were all muddy. She told me that she was going to tell mom on me, but I had nothing to do with her falling down. They were playing around, not me. Ida cried all the way home. When we got home, my parents blamed me for everything that happened. I was tired of this life at home.

I did not tell my mother and father about my plans. I was going to see to it that I was going to make things work. So the next Sunday, I got ready for this guy. I told Wilbert that if he wanted to continue to see me, he had to wear better clothes. He dressed better after that.

Well, he asked me to marry him again. I said, "Yes." Since he was much older, I thought he knew more about life. Boy, was I wrong! This man did not know anything about responsibilities. He made a mess of everything. Wilbert did not know how to heat water. I found out what he wanted in life and what he wanted was a good time ... but not with me!

When we first got married in 1945, he did not have a job, and I worked for a Preacher. Wilbert was lazy, and he worked only a few days out of a week. He made just enough money to buy a little bit of groceries. Some days, he did nothing but sleep all day. We were forced to move in with my brother Elliott.

After a while, Wilbert found steady work. Elliott and my husband bought a basket of sweet potatoes. My sister-in-law would not share the sweet potatoes. This kind of conflict continued for some time. I was tired living in the house with my brother. We had very little privacy.

One day, my husband said to me, "Let's take a walk." As we walked along the railroad tracks, he was making plans. He said, "Luwenia, let's try to get our own house, because we need be to ourselves." I think that my husband had a feeling that his sister was taking over. We went back to the house. I liked the plans and that made me work harder.

Later, I found out that I was "in the family way" (pregnant) with my first child, so I stayed with my brother waiting for my baby to be born. When I told Wilbert, he did not act like the same man that was making plans along the railroad tracks. He did not make any effort to follow through with the plans. He did nothing. I was the only one trying to make ends meet. He acted like I was supposed to be the bread-winner in the family, actually I was.

Wilbert changed so much that I did not know him anymore. Then, he began to stay out nights. When night came, he was getting his clothes ready to go out for the next day. Moving to myself sounded pretty good at this point of our marriage. When he did not do anything to make life better for us, I finally took over. He was threatened to straighten up and accept his share of the load or I would leave him.

That was said so many times before until he did not believe me anymore. I accepted odd jobs waiting for him change. When he did not improve, I knew he needed help. I believed something was wrong with his mind. How could two men be so different? I often thought about how kind Jared was to me, and how Wilbert was so mean? But, God planned it that way, I guess.

The only thing that Wilbert wanted to do was to be with his friends and drink. His drinking was out of control. When he went out on a Friday night, he would come back in Monday morning. I was in a mess, but I kept my mind in the right place. No matter what happened, I was not going to trust this man, so I kept my eyes open.

All kind of thoughts rushed through my mind. I thought, what would happen if he started fighting? I grew up knowing that my father would not allow his children to fight each other. Mom and dad never fought the whole time I was home. What was I to do? I was going to make the best of my situation. Wilbert was stronger than I was, but, if he came towards me to fight, I was not going to stand there and allow him to hit me. I was not going to say what I would or would not do. But, I was not afraid of him.

Chapter Four

Death Claims First Born

After my first baby was born in September 1946, Ida named her Elaine. Elaine was a very pretty little girl with long hair. I could wash her hair and it would touch her shoulders. Most black baby's hair would curl after washing, but not hers. Wilbert did not like holding babies, even his own.

When she was three months old, I laid her down with a bottle of milk for the night. That was the last time I saw my beautiful baby alive. She died during the night. She did not stay with me long. My sister nearly died herself when she found out that I had lost Elaine. The baby was her heart (the love of her life). She died in December of 1946.

Oh God! I almost died when I lost Elaine! I was only 19 years old! I lost so much weight that I only weighed 99 pounds. It was hard trying to start my life over without my baby. I went to the doctor and he put me on a special diet. I had no money to buy these things. So, I tried working again. I made $5.00 a day and that didn't go far at all.

I had a lot to think about in my life. I felt like it was all work and no-o-o joy. I was fed up! But what could I do? I had no clothes, nothing in the house to sit on, and no table to even place a lamp. This man that I married could care less for what I wanted in life.

When my first child died, I found out that I was already two months pregnant with my second child. We moved from the house by the railroad tracks to Mr. Clyde Hogan's house near the church. After *death claims* my *first born*, Wilbert became a brutal man. A few months into our new home, I received my first slap across the face from him. I

29

was so hurt that I only cried. He had really changed for the worst. He never said anything to me about Elaine, but I believe he blamed me for the death of our child.

Mr. Hogan, a white friend of dads, saw how my husband was treating me, and he told daddy to get me out of that mess. The living conditions were bad. There were three different families living in the same house, including my mother-in-law. The other couples fussed and fought all night long. It was a mess living in that house and so was my life!

I remembered one night after saying my prayers; I got into bed and fell asleep. I was suddenly awakened. Just about 2 o'clock in the morning, it seemed like something was looking at me. I looked up and there was a big ring of white flower trimmed in gold sitting in the middle of the ceiling. I sat up and stared at the ceiling. It was still there. I thought that I was seeing things.

I tried to wake up my husband by shaking him. I shook him again to show him the beautiful flowers. But all he did was pulled the covers over his head. He said, "Luwenia, you don't see nuttin', go back to sleep you are dreaming!" But I knew better. Deep down in my heart, I knew that God was showing me that he was with me, no matter what. My husband said, "Don't show me nuttin' else!" I know what I saw.

Just before the second baby was born, I began to see more things. I went to bed early one night because I was not feeling well. I fell asleep and woke up to see three people standing at the foot of my bed. Each of them had a bright ring about their heads like the sun. One was tall, there was one of medium height, and the last one was short. It frightened me so badly I called my husband. As soon as I called his name, he jumped out of bed and ran outside in his underwear. I sat straight up in bed. I did not go back to sleep any more that night. It was a confusing night.

Almost nine months pregnant with my second child, I came from the outside onto the porch. Just as I stepped onto the porch to open the back door, Wilbert grabbed one of my legs, pulled me off the porch, and twirled me around really fast. I screamed to him to let go of my leg. He got worse and that's when I got angry. When he saw that I was getting angry, he let go of my leg, ran in the house, and locked the door. He acted like he wanted me to lose the baby.

There was an axe near the back door, so I grabbed the axe and threw it through the door. I could hear him running down the hall to the front door. When I was able to get inside, my husband ran outside into the middle of the field next to the house. As I reached the front door he yelled back to me, "I hope God to kill me, I promise not to do that anymore!"

I went to stay with daddy for a while to get away and to go to work. Many of my things were left at the house. Daddy was mad about what I had told him, he said let him come around here starting trouble. I went back to the house for some of my things. I met my sister-in-law at the door. She married my brother Elliott plus she was Wilbert's sister. Wilbert left orders to let no one into the bedroom when he was not home. I told her to move out of my way or when I come back to get my other things, I will bring the *law*. She said, "You don't have to do all that."

Wilbert promised to do better and I went back home with him. That was a mistake, because he still stayed out nights. Two to three weeks after that incident, he was out having fun, and I was home alone in pain all night. When Wilbert finally made it home the next morning and saw me in pain, he went to get the midwife. A few hours later, my son, Wayne was born in that house on May 1947, a big baby weighing ten pounds.

It was very cold in that house. We had no wood and I had to go outside to get to my bedroom. The baby was placed on my bed as I went to find some wood to make a fire. My bay had gotten cold and started to cry. By that time I knew Wayne was going to be sick. The baby was only six months old and he cried all night. The next morning, my brother gave me a ride to the doctor's office. He was diagnosed as having double pneumonia.

Wilbert and I moved out of that house with all those people. We moved away from everybody, to "Nine Foot Road" (had something to do with the way roads were made). We had no electricity, no running water, and no heat. I found out that I was *in the family way* with my third child. I had a baby and I was carrying one, again.

Strange things kept happening to me everywhere we lived. For example, I was almost finished cooking one day and needed more wood from the woodpile. As I was about to pick up some wood, a black snake moved. The way his back looked, it was coming towards me. I could not see the head, only the tail. When you are seven months pregnant, you can't run fast. By the time I got to the house and sat down on the porch to rest, the snake was there too. Rolling over backwards onto the porch in much pain, I got up and went into the house closing the door behind me. Looking outside through the crack of the door, the snake had wrapped itself around the pump and was whipping it.

I thought I was going to have that baby that night. After two weeks, the pain eased. It was time for the baby to be born, so I told Wilbert that I needed to buy a few things for the baby. I could not buy much because money was scarce. When we got to the store, Wilbert stayed in the car waiting for me to finish shopping.

While walking towards the store, I noticed a white man and woman walking together. As they approached me, I moved over to one side, at least I tried to get to one side. When I moved over, they did too. They were laughing and coming right towards me. I said, "Oh my God, these people are trying to hurt me."

When the man got close to me, he brought up his knee and with great force, pushed it into my stomach. Entering the store holding my stomach, I was in tears. The people in the store saw when the man and woman hurt me on the street. Hurrying towards me, they asked me was I all right? I said yes. They said, "That was a mean thing to do. Do you want us to call the ambulance?" "No," I said slowly. I was in so much pain that I could barely walk. The way the car was parked, Wilbert could not see anything. I finally made it back to the car, got in, and told him about what happened in front of the store. He didn't say much.

When we got home, Wilbert asked me what did I do to those people. I said, "Nothing." Crying all night because of the pain, it was hard to understand why those people did that to me. I had never seen them before in my life, but it came to me. It was the devil in them. I said to myself, "I'll see them again one day."

Nine months pregnant, I went into the field and picked only 12 crates of beans. When the day ended, I went to the store and bought a little bit of groceries (cheese, canned fish, etc.) for Wayne and me. We were staying at mom's house. That same night, pain was shooting in all directions, which gave me signs that it was time. As Wilbert went for the doctor, I took a bath, combed my hair, and place paper on mom's bed in preparation of my child's birth. It was September 1948 when my little boy was born. He was named Clinton, after my brother. Within two weeks, Wilbert asked, "Do you want to go home, now?" I was ready to go because mom let my brother, Jerome eat all my food.

Little over a year later, I found myself pregnant with the fourth child. As my two sons grew up, they were very poor and thin because we did not have much of anything, especially food. But even in our poorest of times, I managed to get the boys a few toys. I bought Wayne a tricycle for Christmas and he kept it for long time before he could ride it.

I had three tubs of water sitting outside on the ground right next to the porch to catch rain (water). The pump water was rusty brown, and my clothes would be the same color. As Wayne was riding his tricycle, he kept riding from one end of the porch to the other. He was enjoying himself so much that he did not pay any attention to the tubs of water. The next thing I knew, he ran off the porch and into a tub of water. My, you could hear him crying all over the neighborhood! I helped Wayne out of the water and placed the tricycle on the porch.

Clinton got a wagon for Christmas. He never said that he wanted to ride Wayne's tricycle. As soon as the tricycle was placed on the porch, he jumped on it. He rode it like he'd been riding it for a long time. Before I could move any of the tubs, Clinton fell in a tub of water, too. I was so shocked. I couldn't believe it, two accidents in one day.

Things were happening so fast, it was hard for me to think of what to do next. Both of them stood wet looking at the tubs of water. I hated to pour out the water so I got the dirty clothes together and washed them. That way I could put up the tubs because I did not know when it was going to happen again. They could have drowned; but God spared us one more time.

One morning, the children and I got up to find nothing in the house to eat but a little bit of leftover beef hash. Before Wilbert went to work, he said, "Don't nobody eat that beef hash. I want that for my dinner." He didn't care about anybody else, just as long as he ate. He fussed every day about everything.

I had two boys and six months along with my fourth child and nothing to eat. I was sitting on the chair wondering how I was going to feed my children. All at once, there were three knocks on the side of the house. I went to the door, looked down on the porch, and there laid two geese with their heads cut off. They were hanging off the edge of the porch so the blood could run onto the ground. Someone took the time to even think of that. I said, "My Lord, what is this?" I rushed outside, looked all around the house, and saw no one. It was hard to believe what was happening.

I took the geese, picked off the feathers, and looked around for something sharp. With no decent knife to cut out the guts, I picked up a piece of broken glass and started cutting, which did not work well. I soon found a half of a knife inside the house, sharpened it on the bricks, and cleaned the geese.

I took a lard *stand* and put water in it. There was no wood to make a big fire to cook, but I gathered lots of chips to keep the fire going. Finding four bricks, I placed them in a box shape and pushed the chips of wood inside of it. The fire was started on the ground. The lard *stand* was placed over the fire onto the bricks. A big fire was made so the geese could continue to boil.

Finally, the geese were done enough to eat. I had no pan to put the broth in, for that reason I used a wash pan. The pan was cleaned outside with some sand and soap. It was washed and rinsed at the pump, and the broth was poured into the pan. A few leftover lumps of flour found in the sifter were used to make the gravy. With the rest of the chips, a big fire was made in the stove to brown the geese in the oven.

After they were browned, I took them out of the oven, sliced one of them, and gave a piece to my oldest son Wayne. He sat on the floor and not a word was said. He just sat there with is head hanging down. Just as soon as I gave him the food, he started cramming food in his mouth with both hands. He was so hungry that he started choking on the food. I told him to take his time eating. That child ate two plates full of food before he calmed down. While feeding Clinton, he stopped and stared at his brother.

Their daddy came home after work asking for his beef hash. I told him, "There it is on the table." He looked on the stove and asked, "What's that?" I said, "Geese." He asked, "Where did you get them geese from?" I said, "I don't know." He said, "Luwenia (He could never say my name right.), don't stand there acting like a fool." I said, "I really don't know where they came from. I heard three knocks on the side of the house. I went outside and the geese were on the porch." God said that He will feed His children, and that's what He did; fed his children.

Chapter Five

Husband Leaves Home

In the spring of 1950, we moved close to the water on Lakeside and my fourth child was born shortly after. I named the baby boy Rodney. He was a crying baby, even after he was older. The house was beautiful with fruit trees in the yard. Even though the house was pretty, we had no electricity, no running water, and no heat again. I listened to the morning devotion every day on a battery radio. This preacher ended his program everyday by saying, "I'll see you tomorrow." The radio would be turned off a few seconds after that message, because we could not afford a new battery.

One day after the man said that, I heard some loud music, but the radio was turned off. "Where is this music coming from?" I thought it was coming from my friend's house, so I went over there. But, it was not coming from there either. I came back through the house, went out in the yard, and looked up towards the sky.

Oh my God! What a beautiful sight! The sky was painted with all the colors of the rainbow. Angelic music rang across the heavens with a harp softly playing in the background. Where I was standing, if I had lifted up one foot I think would have gone right up in the clouds. I did not know what this meant.

I called out to my husband who was working to the barn at the time. The barn was not far from the house. Excited about the clouds, I called to him several times. He finally came out. When I was showing it to him, he didn't see it. So I pointed to the sky. He never did see it. Those beautiful clouds were fading and rolling away across the sky. He called me crazy, but I knew what I saw.

Desperate to feed the children, I sent my oldest son Wayne to the store at five years old. It was only a short distance down the road. I was getting ready to have my fifth child. I could not walk very far, so I pinned a note on Wayne's coat and sent him to the store. The note told the storekeeper what I wanted, one pound of sugar and ½ pound of salt meat.

He stayed so long until I said to myself, "Let me go find that child." I lived back off the road and the pasture nearly surrounded the yard with a double fence. In order to get to the road, I had to go through two gates. I climbed to the top of the fence because the boss man locked one of them. Reaching the top, I saw trouble! Wayne was throwing rocks at the cows. He was spooking the cows into a stampede but he didn't know it. I whistled through my two fingers to get his attention. He looked at me. I yelled very loudly, "Come on here, Hurry! Hurry! Hurry up!" He started running towards me.

It was a bridge that I had to cross before I could get to the fence. At the top of the fence, I could see the cows trotting right behind him. He came to me in the knick of time. I said, "Hold the bag of food." I took him up in my arms. As soon as we got off the gate, all the cows bumped into the fence. I walked as fast as I could to the last fence. When we went through the last gate and fastened it, it gave me time to get inside the yard.

Safely inside the house, I took the bag and looked at the note that the storekeeper pinned on Wayne's coat. It read. "If you ever send that little boy to my store again, I am going to have you arrested." I did not send him to the store anymore. You see he was only five and we were desperate for food.

We had been in the house for three years when Wayne got sick again. He was outside pulling on a cows tail when all at once he started coughing. I was on my knees scrubbing the floor and heard him crying. Stopping to hear what was going on, I slowly walked to the door. Surprisingly, Wayne was crying and coughing up blood. Frightened, I ran to him and picked him up in my arms. Unsure of what to do, I ran inside and tried everything to calm him down. His condition worsened during the night which prompted me to get his clothes ready for the next morning.

Before daybreak, Wayne and I was dressed and ready for the long walk to the doctor's office. It was Sunday morning and Wilbert was nowhere to be found. The death of my first-born flashed before me as I watched Wayned gasping for air. "Dear God! This cannot be happening to me again." There was no telephone or transportation. Wilbert had not been home in two days. Forced to leave the other children home, I left the house walking with Wayne in my arms, wrapped, in a blanket. Every step was made in desperation of saving my child's life. When I got to Marvin Street, the doctor stared at me in a strange way. He asked, "What's the matter with him?" It was nice and warm in his office. I told him and he asked me to take off his clothes. He instructed me to place him on the examining table. While gently pressing the stethoscope to his chest, he asked me how did I get to his office. I said, "I walk." He seemed shocked that I had walked approximately 5 miles with Wayne in my arms, but I had no other choice. With concern, he told me to take the baby home because he had double pneumonia again. He gave some medicine and told me to take good care of him. Lord! I cried all the way home. The other children were all right when we returned home. I couldn't thank the Lord enough when Wayne was no longer sick.

Phyllis was born at Lakeside in February 1952. She was a beautiful, quiet baby and she didn't give me a moment of trouble. Wilbert left me alone many nights. He was always gone somewhere, but he was home long enough to keep me pregnant! I was having children one after the other. Fifteen months after my fifth child, I was "in the family way" again.

One night in 1953, I was at church singing with the group on the front seat. Terry, the man who attacked me when I was 14, came to church. I was twenty-six years old then. Terry was coming up the back stairs. I asked myself what must I do? On the way to church, I found a pocket knife. Something said you are on your way to church, why do you need a knife?

As I was going downstairs, he said to me, "Yeah, there you go. Now I'm going to finish the job I started a long time ago." I told him, "I was a little girl at that time, I'm a grown woman now. I can handle you all by myself." By that time, one of the deacons of the church came in and asked what was going on. He said to Terry, "Get away from this church and let these people alone." Since that night, I saw him one more time. He died soon after that.

I knew Wilbert was with other women, but I never suspected that he wanted me out of his life so badly. He was working on the farm, and he came home one day at lunchtime with a box of cereal in his hand. I was in the kitchen cooking. As soon as he reached me the box, he went back to work. Wilbert never brought food home, which made me suspicious. I was suspicious, but I did not discern his motives. *Something said, "do not eat that."* I told the children do not eat it. They said, "Why mom?" I said, "I am going to eat a little bit first, then I will let you try it." I put a little in my hands. No sooner than I put it in my mouth, it started to burn my mouth and stomach as it went down. My head started spinning around, and I passed out on the floor.

When I woke up, I told Wayne to bring me some milk, which he did. It stopped the burning in my stomach, but I kept passing out. My son gave me milk 5 to 6 more times.

After a while, the fainting spell left me. I do not know what was in that cereal, but it made me sick. I threw the rest of the cereal away so the children would not eat any of it.

As my husband returned home from work that evening, I saw him come up to the porch very slowly. He stood there picking at his nose and hesitating to come inside. He acted so suspicious that he gave himself away. I said, "Come in. I am not dead yet. I know you tried to do something to me with that cereal. I am going to have you arrested." He was so afraid that he went across the field running. I did not see him anymore that day.

I had no proof, but I believed he was trying to kill me. I made up my mind that I would never accept any more food from him. I continued to watch him for a long time. If he had any left over food, it would be thrown out, because I was afraid to eat any of it.

A few months later, I was weak and felt sick all the time. My husband said, "Luwenia, get the children ready, we're going to Belleview." I did not go anywhere much, so I liked the idea and got the children ready. We left to pick up his mother and one of his sisters. I was six months pregnant with my sixth child. I was tired of riding, but I hung right in there.

Wilbert finally pulled up to this unknown place. I knew something was wrong because the place did not look like a house and it did not look like an office either.

Things just didn't feel right. My husband told me that something was wrong with me. I knew nothing was wrong with me. I was "saved" and he was not. He couldn't understand it.

We went to the door. The man talked slowly and holding his words a long time. "Come in and have a seat," he said. All of a sudden something came across my mind. This man must be a fortuneteller! Wilbert said something was wrong with me so he brought me to this man. He

41

didn't let me know why he was bringing me here. But, in my heart, I prayed to God, "Lord, take care of me."

As I went in and sat down, he asked my husband, "What can I do for you?"

Wilbert said, "I want you to look at my wife." The man asked him, "Does she fight you?" "No," he said. Then his mother said, "She just doesn't treat him right." The man told Wilbert, "Take your wife home and feed her. She needs food. She is getting ready to have a baby and you're bringing her to me?" I took the children back to the car. My husband stayed in the office with the man. I think the man felt I was with God.

On the way back home, oh my God, didn't my husband fuss! He fussed about how the man did not tell him what he wanted to hear. He wanted the man to say I was crazy, but it didn't work. Then, his mother and sister fussed at me too, but it didn't matter. My mind was made up. I was going to stay with God.

A few weeks later, Wilbert took me to his uncle's house. He had three uncles and one aunt. I still did not know what he planned to do. I prayed all the way there. Finally, we arrived at his uncle's house and they met us at the door. I don't know what my husband told them before I got there.

We went inside. They looked at me as though I was someone they had never seen before. They said, "Let us pray." We prayed. After we finished praying, they asked me, "Are you saved?" I said, "Yes." "Why don't you go to church?" I said, "Because I don't have any clothes." They told Wilbert that he had on nice clothes. Why couldn't he get some clothes for the children and me and take us to church? One of his uncles told my mother-in-law, "Sis, you and your son need to go to God." Wilbert and his mother left their relatives upset. My husband went back to his uncle's house one more time. After that, he never went back because they didn't tell him what he wanted to hear.

Wilbert wanted his mother to help me after the baby was born. I told him that I didn't want her to come over. He brought her over anyway. To get away from them, I ran out the back door and jumped over the fence. Boy! Was I in pain! Chasing after me, my husband called out to me in a distance. "Luwenia! Luwenia! Come back here, you crazy fool!" A few steps from the fence, I felt something running down my legs.

I was soon rushed to the hospital and in January 1954, my sixth child was born. She was a beautiful baby and resembled Elaine. Her head was full of curls and we called her Maggie. While in the hospital, I learned that the baby had attached itself to the wall of my womb, which explained my troublesome pregnancy. When I returned home from the hospital, it was one of the coldest winters I had ever seen in my life. Wilbert, my five children, and I slept in one bed.

I said to myself, I've got to do something. I asked my sister Beatrice to keep my children for me when Maggie was six months old. She said she would. I heard that a person could make a lot of money in New York picking potatoes and pickles. The people who took me to New York to harvest crops had been going for years. This was my first time. After paying my way there, I only had seventy-five cents left.

When I got to Long Island, the contractor invited me to stay in one of his labor cottages. The change was used to buy a dozen of eggs and a box of crackers. There was no stove to cook on. I went outside to gather some bricks to build a fire, and put some water in a lard can. This was so familiar to me. I dug up some potatoes, washed them off, and boiled them with some salt and pepper. That was all I had to eat until it was time to work.

It would be two weeks before harvesting started. I asked another contractor about picking pickles for him. He said that he would love to have me working for him. Now, I had two jobs. The days I wasn't picking cucumbers, I would be picking potatoes. The people who took me to New York were selling ½ chicken, two slices of bread, and a little bit of potato chips for $10.00. I could not afford that.

When one of my cousins found out that I had two jobs, she said to me, "You know what, I could really mess up things for you." I asked her, "How's that?" She said, "Up here (meaning New York), you can only work for one man at a time." She didn't have anything on me because I had already gotten that straightened out. She hadn't offered me anything while I was there. It was hard to believe that she was trying to get money out of me too.

I was getting two checks instead of one. Since I left my children with my sister, I was sending money to her every week. Three weeks after I arrived in New York, Wilbert and his brother brought two women with them. My aunt was the one who saw them first. She said, "Lord have mercy. There is Wilbert with another woman." I said, "Where?" She said, "Over there." Just as I was making pretty good money, my husband showed up.

He came straight towards me with that woman. I said, "Why are you here?" He said, "I came to take you back home." I replied, "I am not going anywhere. You didn't bring me up here. What make you think that I will go back home with you? I've come to make some money and that is what I am going to do. If you want to go back home, go ahead. You need to take that skinny-legged woman back where she came from and leave me alone." Wilbert said, "All right now, Luwenia." He refused to leave and found work in the cucumber patch.

My husband didn't want to work, so he worked when he felt like it. One week when the contractor was paying people, he told me that I made $129.00 and Wilbert only made $11.25. The contractor said that he was the laziest man he had ever seen. To cash the check, I went to the store to pick up my lay-a-way. When I came out, I heard

44

my husband say, "My God! That woman went in there and spent all my 'dag doosted' money!" He said, "Luwenia! Give me my 'dag doosted' money!" I said, "Wilbert, the contractor said that you only get $11.25, and that's all you're going to get!"

People knew my husband, and he was known for being a bully. Wilbert was mad about the amount of money he had received for the week. He cursed me so badly that my cousins were afraid for me. One of my aunts asked me if I needed help. I said, "No, because I am not scared of Wilbert. I worked hard for my money, and he better not try anything today!" He soon calmed down. We went our separate ways. I went back to the boarding house to eat dinner.

After I had eaten, washed the dishes, and bathed, I laid down across the bed. Soon as I dozed off to sleep, I had a vision. Jesus said, "Go Home." I got up and walked outside. My aunt asked me if everything was all right. Slowly I answered, "Yes." My thoughts were not clear and I began to ask myself questions. As I went back inside to lie down, the same vision appeared again. The next, day I received a letter from my sister to inform me that my baby was sick. This time I did just like He said; I told Wilbert about Maggie being sick, packed my things, and went home.

I kept wondering what the vision meant on my way home. Wilbert and I took a boat from New York across the Chesapeake Bay in a hurricane, Hazel. The wind was causing the waves to be bigger than normal. The person manning the boat was also a little afraid of the large swollen waves. He let out loud yells, with occasional profanity, as the boat dipped deeply into the bay waters. Leaving the boat, we took a bus home from Virginia.

Our first stop was to pick up the car to get the children. When we arrived at Beatrice's house, I found out my purpose of coming home. Maggie was so sick that she couldn't bend her legs. We took the children home right away. When I tried to stand her up at home, she moaned in pain. It sounded like she was grunting every breath. After filling a tub with hot water, I put in a little bit of alcohol and the baby was placed in the tub. When I first put her in the water, she grunted as if her body was hurting all over.

Almost an hour later, I took her out of the water and placed her down on a clean pillow. She slept all night. When she woke up that next morning, she was very happy. The other children were happy to see that the baby was well and I was back home. Even though I needed the money, I was glad to see them too.

As months went by, my former boss stopped by my house one morning to ask me if I wanted to work. Because I did not have a phone, people had to come to my house just to see if I wanted to work. I said yes. The next morning I got up and all I could see was ice all over the ground.

I asked myself who was going to take care of Maggie, because she was only eleven months old. I had a wood heater in the house. Wayne was seven now, and maybe he could take care of the other children. These people always gave me a lot of good things, and this was a blessing, which made me anxious to work for them. But before I left home, I filled the heater with wood and cut the vent on the stove down. An old big piece of wood was placed in the stove so it would last until I got back. I had no business leaving a little boy in charge of all those children, but I needed a lot of things. I took a chance and told him what to do while I was gone. He was not to put any wood in the heater or cook stove, and what times to give the baby her bottle.

I got down on my knees and prayed to the Lord Jesus, "Please keep my children safe until I get back." Walking all the way to town in the cold, I did not know what to do when I arrived at the house. They wanted me to iron clothes.

When the ironing was done, I was really tired. The man asked, "Louvenia, do you have any room for a bed?" I said, "Oh yes!" He looked at me a long time. He gave me a bed, sheets, and pillows. The man drove a bread truck so he gave me cakes, pies, honey buns, and made me a very happy woman.

When he drove me home with all my things he had given to me, oh, how I thanked God that my children were all right, and I had a bed and food to eat. To top it all off, he paid me $10.00. Ten dollars in those days was a lot of money, to me anyway. The fire had gone down, but not completely out. The children could not play outside so, they taught the baby how to walk. She was crawling about on the floor when I left for work that morning. For the first time in a long time I felt joy.

Wilbert stayed home long enough for me to get *in the family way*, again. Maggie must have been seven months old when I got pregnant. Nine months later in 1955, Amy was born. The owner of the house and the farm threw some white feed bags on the front porch. I took the cotton bags to make my children some shorts, slips, and underwear. These things were sown by hand. I did not have any thread in the house, but I used the thread from the bags to sew the clothes for my children.

Throwing those white bags on the porch was just a way of inviting Wilbert out of the house to talk. His boss offered to sell him the house and take $8.00 out his pay each month if he stayed on the farm. But my husband insisted on going back to New York because he was tired of working on the farm. The farm was a beautiful place to live, especially near the water. I hated to move because it was one of the best places we had ever lived. There were lots of fruit trees and plenty of fish from the river. I was able to raise chickens and have eggs for the children.

My husband told me to go live with my father, because he was not planning on coming back. I said, "I was not going live with my father. He's always taking my money." When I told Wilbert that, he slapped me to the floor and walked out of the door. My *husband left me and* five children with nowhere to go.

Wilbert did not care about how we were going to move out of that house; he just left us with no money or food. My brother helped the children and I move close to my parents. The four–room house had no electricity, no running water and no heat. We moved from Lakeside when Amy was only two weeks old. I took down beds and moved furniture during a very dangerous period after childbirth. Pain was covering every inch of my body. The children and I almost died of starvation. Since we lived so close to my parents, we could walk to their house for food.

I can remember one day I walked to my father's house to get some food. Phyllis was three years old and she wanted some water. She was just as hard-headed as she could be. Before I could get some water, she had already made it to the pump. Daddy had a pump that was made low to the floor. This was a perfect situation for a child her age. I told her to stop pumping because she was getting wet. Daddy said to me, "Leave her alone." Since I was at his house, he wanted me to obey his wishes. I told him, "This is my child." He said, "Go back in the house." I said, "I am not."

He grabbed me and tried to pull me inside the house. I wrapped my arm around a post and he pulled for the longest time. I wouldn't let go of the post. After awhile he gave up and we went home hungry. He wouldn't speak to me for almost a year. I did not look back, and I even stopped going to his house. I was a woman now and he wanted to continue to treat me as his little girl. Times had changed but he had not.

Gus (the owner of the house) planted some white potatoes which the fields surrounded the house. We were so hungry. I dug up some potatoes and cooked them.

Checking on his crops one day, Gus saw what I did. He did not get angry, but he told me not to dig in the middle of the field, instead dig on one side. That was truly a blessing.

Wilbert finally sent a little bit of money home from New York. He came home shortly after and we made up, again. Little did we know that a hurricane was headed our way. We went to my parents' house and stayed all night. When we went back home the next day, the storm had blown a tree over the house. If we had stayed, we probably would have been badly hurt or dead. Gus used a tractor to pull the tree off the house and sawed it up for firewood. We soon used the wood up for cooking and heating.

Wilbert could not find any other work, so he went back to work on the farm for the same man. There were times we did not have wood to burn. We went in the woods and broke up some limbs and branches. I could not sit down and wait for Wilbert to come home. I worked hard trying to keep the house warm. Nights were very cold in that house.

My children used to wet the beds because we didn't have a bathroom. The house was too cold for my children to get up and go to the (pot). When they wet the bed, I could see ice hanging from the sheets. Phyllis would be so wet and cold. I do believe it caused her to have rheumatism in the joints of her knees and hips. She could not walk without a stick or some one to help her. I used to cry many days and nights worrying about my little girl walking across the yard that way. When she wanted to go to the pot she would cry for help, because it hurt her so badly. Even though Wilbert came back home nothing changed.

Maggie was into everything when she was three years old. In the summer of 1957, flies were very bad. I put some fly-poison down in the windowsills. The crystals were very colorful and eye catching to a toddler. Every little pink piece of poison she saw, she ate it. Boy, did she get sick! I didn't know what to do. Some rice was boiled until it was very soft. I placed a piece of thin cloth over the baby's bottle to strain the rice. After it cooled, the baby was given the juice from the rice. Soon as she would drink the rice milk, it went right through her. It scared me. She hardly opened her eyes during most of her sickness. I said, "Lord, please help me."

She had fewer bowel movements within hours, and she opened her eyes. She made improvements everyday. Maggie finally got well. I said, "Thank you Lord for saving my baby." I had no money to carry her to the doctor, but Jesus lead me in the right direction when I prayed to him. I'd never used that poison again.

Chapter Six

Seven Hungry Children

When a house has no electricity, no running water, and no heat, it is hard to manage a small house with my crew. We suffered with no food and clothes because I wasn't working regularly. The pump was broken most of the time.

It seemed like I was never going to bring my head above water. To top it off, Amy was a sickly child. No matter what I would do, she wanted me to hold her all the time. When I went to hang out clothes, she wanted to go too. One day she cried so much that I took her to the doctor to find what was wrong. The doctor told me she had gone into *blood poisoning*. The insects were so bad that I believe that she'd been bitten by something poisonous.

Wilbert stayed out all hours of the night, and I suspected him of cheating on me again. I went looking for him to tell him about the baby. I stopped over to my mom's house and was told that he was at the sandpit with my sister, Sheila! I was shocked to find out that it was true. It hurt me to see my sister in my husband arms. What hurt me even more is what she said when she was caught. "You should keep your husband at home!" She was not the only mistress in his life. He had been sleeping with other women that were related to me as well. Women under garments and wine bottles were found in his car. I saw him for what he was, no good!

I lived across the road from a rich white family that cleaned chickens. Some of them were teachers and they were cleaning chickens for the whole town. She cleaned chickens for schools, stores, restaurants, and many more places. She asked me if I wanted to clean chickens for her. I said, "Yes." I was so excited about getting a job that I did not ask her how much she was going to pay me. I had cleaned chickens all day long, and she paid me only $2.00. I did not go over there anymore. It was time for me to move on. That's when I started cleaning cottages. I went from one thing to another until I found what I wanted to do. I saved my money for hard times.

We lived across the road from another white family. They were very compassionate people who saw how poor we were. Many times I did not have anything in the house to eat. This family brought milk, cereal, and bread to help me feed six children. I was so grateful for their kindness shown towards this black family.

When Maggie was five years old in 1959, I was sick again and had worked so hard that the doctor told me not work in the fields anymore. Again, I needed money badly. I did not get any money until I worked for it. My husband kept all his money for himself.

One morning, I was sick at home and every time I would stand up, I fainted. It was very cold in the house, so I asked my son, Rodney to make a fire in the stove. He said, "I can't find a match." I told him to look down in the stove for hot ashes. He did. He took a little piece of paper and started putting the paper on the coal and blew on it. He blew and blew. Finally, the fire caught.

Maggie and Amy were helping him to blow on the hot coal with the paper. The smaller one had not played in fire before until that day. When Rodney left the kitchen, they had the playing *blues*. Amy picked up the paper and blew on it, the fire caught onto Maggie's T-shirt. Just as I shouted for them to come to me, Maggie screamed!

Both of them came running through the house. I was sitting by the door when Maggie came by me running with her T-shirt on fire. Unable to stand up because of my sickness, I grabbed the flaming T-shirt with my left hand.

The fire burned my hand, but I didn't let go until the flames were out. Amy was so upset. She began to cry just as much as Maggie.

As sick as I was, I mustered enough strength to walk to my father's house for help. Maggie cried all the way. My father mixed alum and petroleum together. This mixture would heal a burn on anything. I worked on that burn until she fell asleep. Later, we went back home with some of the mixture and I worked on that burn for days. I never gave up no matter how hard things seemed. Soon Maggie was her old self again.

While at home and could not work, I took music lesson so I could learn how to play the piano. When I made a mistake, the music teacher hit me across the fingers. That made me very angry and I never went back for anymore lessons. I taught myself how to play the piano. Hours after hours, I played the piano every chance I got.

Rodney was in his own little world at times and, he was very hard to predict because he was so quiet. He had a B-B gun. He went around the house shooting at everything. As he was shooting up a tree, his little sister, Amy, told him to stop shooting at those birds. He told her to leave him alone or he will shoot her in the forehead. Of course Amy dared him, "You better not, I am going to tell." As she pressed her face against the screen in the window, he shot her in the forehead through the screen. It was so deep that I had to pick it out with a safety pin. Soon as you would look at Rodney straight, he would cry. He really got a spanking from me that day. He did not use that gun anymore. It felt like it was happening all over again (just like my brother Jerome).

As if that wasn't bad enough, he got his head caught between two boards in a small ditch and could not get out. I was so afraid. Oh my God! What was I to do? I could not go and get any help, because we lived so far from the highway. By the time I got back, he would have been dead.

I had heard stories about how people could lift more than their actual weight when tragedy happens. I prayed to God to give me strength. He gave me enough to pull the two boards apart. When Rodney was finally free, he was hurting so badly that he could not cry. I had a belt waiting for him so I could spank him. He looked so pitiful; I let him get by that time.

During the summer months, I took the oldest children out to the fields every day to make some money. Although the doctor restricted me from the fields, we picked potatoes, cut cabbage, and picked cotton. We had to find a way to survive. We worked from sun up to sun down. This was hard work, but I was thankful that I didn't have any lazy children. We did everything together.

Children will be whatever you teach them to be. That was my husband's biggest problem. His mother didn't make him work. He stayed at home or worked whenever he felt like it. He got mad with me because I wanted something out of life, and because we were going on without him. When we made money, he wanted a part of it. He fussed if he didn't get part of the money. The children needed clothes and so many other things to go to school.

When I was younger, my brothers and sisters sang together at church, home, and other places. As I got older, my sisters and I started singing gospel songs as a group. Our group was called the "Riddick Sisters." Since I worked so hard, I found joy in singing gospels. After rehearsal one night, my sister and her husband took me home. They put me out at the highway because the path was full of mud holes and they didn't want to get stuck.

I got out of the car and started walking down the long path. It was so dark that I could not see and I was afraid of stepping on a snake. With each step, the mud covered my shoes.

All at once, the moon came out (I thought it was the moon at that time). The light was so bright that I could even see the ditch bank. I was singing and still hadn't noticed what happened. At last, I made my way to the house. As I stepped inside the house, the light disappeared. I then realized what had happened. God had shown a light for me so that I could see.

As I started to fall backwards, I caught myself. Instead of falling backwards, I started feeling dizzy and fell flat on my face. I fell so hard that I jarred the floor. I landed beside my son who was lying on the floor at the time. I thought I was going to be sore the next day, but I wasn't. This was another mysterious sign from God. That's why I have learned to love and trust Him through the years.

Every Christmas season a man and his wife came by my house with birds and hunting dogs. The house sat in the middle of a very large field. They used the farmland to exercise their hunting dogs. He would let the birds out, shoot them, and the dogs fetched them. After hunting, they gave the birds to me to eat. Sometimes I didn't want them because they were messy to clean. They also gave large bags of candy, pecans, and all kinds of goodies for my children. My children even called him *Mr. Good Man*. After awhile, they didn't come by anymore. We really missed them.

My children were getting much older now and they were able to stay by themselves without any trouble. If I left the house after the children, I left instructions on paper. The notes told them where I was and what time I would be back. Amy was the youngest child at the time, and she got the idea from me of leaving notes. We used cardboard for windowpanes. That's where I would leave my notes. One day, Amy wrote a note on the cardboard. She told a great big fib. The note stated, "Go to grandma's house." The children went to my mother's house. I did not know anything about it. Nobody was at my mother's house so they came back home.

When I got home, I noticed that the girls had on clean clothes, but their hair hadn't been combed. I began to ask questions. I asked my oldest son, "Who told y'all to go to my mother's house? He said, "Amy did". I was very upset. I spanked her little legs for telling a fib and scaring me. She never did that again.

Clinton really could build things. While I was gone to work one summer day, he went to the trash pile across the field behind our house. The trash pile was near a high school. He found lumber and brought it back to the house.. With those boards and an old wheel from a bike, he made a cart to push his sisters and brothers on it one a time. They showed the pushcart to me when I got back, and the children rode on that thing for weeks until it fell apart. He wasn't suppose to go to the trash-pile because it was dangerous. I made a trip to the pile and found a table and a metal wash pan. These two pieces became part of our household furnishings.

The children didn't have any money, so they thought of other ways of getting things they like by saving "Lucky Stars" labels that were on packs of notebook paper. The larger the packs, the more points you would receive. The boys had saved enough "stars" to get a bicycle and a white radio. They were happy about that bicycle, but we couldn't play the radio because there was no electricity.

Having no electricity made me think about my life. I had six children that needed food and clothing. Some white families were still giving me things for the children. It was six years since my last child, and I found out that I was "pregnant" again.

Eight months later, I wasn't feeling well and I caught a ride to the hospital. They kept me for five days because the baby was coming early. I could go home, but no one came to pick me up. I left the hospital on foot and walked approximately 5 miles to my parents. On the way, blood trickled down my legs and I was rushed back to the hospital by my daddy just in the knick of time. I lost so much blood that I needed a blood transfusion, but I had a rare blood type. Therefore, they had to locate a blood donor, which I later found out was a white male.

During my stay, my condition worsened to the point of death, both my child and I. The doctor asked me whose life to save, child's or mine. Of course, I chose my child's life. Miraculously, we both lived! My beautiful little girl was born on December 23, 1961. They watched her for a while, and I had to leave her there. Eventually she was soon released from the hospital to go home. Here we were living in a four-room house and *seven hungry children*. The baby slept in a box for a crib. This was not enough room for nine people and I told Wilbert to look for another house. Although Wilbert was reluctant to move, I encouraged him to find antoher house.

It was near Christmas time and Phyllis drew candles and Christmas trees in the windows with crayons. The boys laughed and said, "No one is going to see those candles from here." She said, "I know that. But, at least the people that come by our yard will know that we care about Christmas." They stopped laughing and began to draw candles themselves.

Chapter Seven

The House with Electricity

In January 1962, when Carla was 2 weeks old, we moved to a larger house. It had six rooms downstairs and two rooms upstairs. Like the other houses, there were no electricity, no running water, and no heat. The three boys, Wayne, Clinton, and Rodney shared one bedroom and Phyllis, Maggie, and Amy shared the other. The baby (Carla) slept with us. I really started seeing a difference in my life.

Within a few months after we moved, the baby started coughing a little. Later that night, she had a fever. I could tell, because her skin was dry and very hot. She became very cranky and fussy. She started to breathe funny, and I told Wilbert that we better take her to the hospital right away. I am glad we did because the doctor told us that the baby had pneumonia. I believe she became sick because the house was large; we couldn't keep it warm enough for the baby. The doctor gave me some medicine for Carla and told me to keep an eye on her. In several days, she was better.

My children had to a give report on current events daily. In the spring of that year, I was tired of my children going to school and not having any news. I wanted my children to be like other children. We didn't have any electricity, and kerosene lamps were the source of light to do their homework. They could barely see what they were writing. I made up my mind to turn on the electricity that day, and I did. I found the brightest bulb in an electric lamp and we all shared that one lamp. That was one of the happiest nights of our lives.

When Wilbert came home that night, he was furious. We fought and fought that night. He knew he wasn't going to turn on the electricity himself, but he was upset because I did. He did not want to spend his money on electricity. He said that I was wasting money. I really got mad when he told me that he was going to turned off the electricity. I said, "If you touch those lights, I was going to kick you all over the house." Even though he was mean, I wasn't scared of him. It stayed on and, it didn't take long for him to learn the benefits of electricity. He enjoyed having the radio on every morning before he left for work. As a matter fact, he used the same radio the children and I saved from the "Lucky Stars." This is was the first time we lived in a *house with electricity*.

At one point, he claimed the radio to be his own and this highly upset the children and me. We had an argument over the radio. He would not allow anyone to change the station, and he threatened to "bust" up the radio. When this happened, my oldest son Wayne, at the age of 15, came in the room where I was. He asked me, "Mom, why are you letting daddy have his way all the time? You don't let the children do that. Why do you keep having children for daddy? You know he doesn't love you." I was cleaning up at the time and I stopped because he'd never asked me anything like that before. What was going across his mind? I asked myself could this be true? After he said that, I knew it was time to make some *changes*.

One night as I was giving the baby a bath. We were laughing and playing. He asked me why was I laughing so much. He said, "That's all right, you will be pregnant again in a few months." I said, "What did you say? I thought to myself. *You wanted me to be pregnant all this time to keep me down. I see. Why am I having children for this man? He's just like a beast.* That conservation really opened my eyes and made me get a grip of myself. Even my children knew what kind of man he was!

The next night, I moved out of his bedroom into another room to myself. He was very upset when we slept in separate rooms. I had to be on guard every night and day trying to keep him from hurting me. I did not know what to expect of him.

Sleeping in my bed one night, I felt very strange. Something told me to move my feet to the other side of the bed, but I did not move them right away. Then, a voice said, again, move your feet to the other side of the bed! I carried a knife or ice pick to bed with me to protect myself. As soon as I moved my feet, something hit the bed. I could not see what it was in the dark but it scared me. His intentions were to hurt me, *badly*.

In the dark, I reached for the knife and I struck at him ... I thought. When I turned on the lights, he was just standing there. I noticed a small cut on his arm. Surprised he said, "You are *toting* a weapon for me, huh?" I replied, "You dog gone right!" As I jumped out of bed and started towards him, he ran down the hall through the living room to his bedroom. He did not bother me any more that night.

People used to come to our house and find us fighting like cats and dogs. When I went to church, people used to stare at me because sometimes my clothes were torn. Some of the things we used to fight about were women, money and jealousy (of me talking with the children).

I remembered early one very cold spring, all the children except the oldest girl (Phyllis) were sitting around a wood heater trying to keep warm. Phyllis came inside running and yelling, "The house is on fire!" At first I didn't believe it until I saw fire coming down from the ceiling in the kitchen.

I told some of the children to take the furniture and put them in the front yard. One of them went to the neighbor's house to use the phone to call the fire department. The neighbor and others used buckets of pumped water to put out the fire. We didn't have a ladder, but the neighbor climbed to the roof and threw buckets of water on the fire. It was out by the time the firemen got there. The owner fixed the roof of the house, but the ceiling inside the house was left undone.

During the first summer at the house, everybody went to work except the girls. They were left to take care of the baby and to do their chores. A cornfield totally surrounded the house with nothing to see or do. After they finished their chores, the girls started drawing and one of the needed a pencil. So, Phyllis started upstairs to get a pencil. On the way upstairs, she glanced at something lying on the steps. Phyllis wondered what it was. At first, she thought it was a black belt. She took another quick glance and realized that it was not a belt but a black snake! She ran back to the other sisters and screaming, "It's a snake in the house!" Amy picked up the baby from the floor and they all ran outside. Amy ran around the house three times. Phyllis told the girls to stay on the porch while she goes to the neighbor's house to get help. As she started down the path, Amy jumped off the porch with the baby in her arms.

When the girls and the neighbor went inside the house to get rid of the snake, he could not find it. They looked on the steps and under the dirty clothes. The neighbor finally found and killed the snake. This made the girls nervous because we did not have any idea how the snake got inside.

When I got home from work, they told me the story. I searched the spare room and the upstairs bedrooms to see how the snake got inside. When I checked out the staircase and the loft, I found a large hole at the top of the staircase. I tore open a small box and covered the hole with it. The girls were afraid to go to bed that night. It took a long time for them to get used to sleeping upstairs again.

The next day, the baby was whining. She couldn't move her arms and legs. She cried when someone picked her up. I couldn't figure out what was wrong. Then it dawned on me. Amy had jumped off the porch with the baby the day before. I gave her a warm bath and rubbed her down with alcohol to remove the stiffness in her limbs. The baby showed improvement by end of the day.

In the summer of 1963, it was a terrible electrical storm. It was thundering and lightning every few minutes. Lord, that was a storm! The lightning struck an electrical transformer beside our house. All the lights went out in the neighborhood. During the storm, a speeding driver hit something in the dark. We heard a loud noise and tires squealing. Later we heard sirens of an ambulance. We could only see shadows as the lightning flashed and flashing red lights.

The day after the accident, my husband came home after work and told us what had happened. He said that the neighbor's horses broke down the fence during the storm and ran into the highway. A teenager was driving the car that hit one of the horses. The young boy came out all right, but the horse died.

That same summer, an insurance representative came to the house to collect payment for the insurance. I told him that I did not have the money to keep it up-to-date. He told me that he would have to elapse it. It hurt me to do that, but I had no other choice. When the insurance man brought the check two months later, my husband saw it. He was being nice and polite, which was very unusual. I knew he had something up his sleeves besides his arm. Wilbert said, "Luwenia, can I borrow that money to pay down on a car for us? I'll pay you back." We did not have a car at that time, so it sounded reasonable. He did use the word "us." I was hesitant at first, then I said, "Okay." He came back with a 1958 light blue Pontiac. He did not pay me back nor did he carry us anywhere.

Days, weeks, and months went by and he still did not take us anywhere in the new car. I waited time after time.

This made me very angry. He hadn't changed his mind. "Wilbert, if you do not give us a ride in that car, I am going to tear it into pieces." He went out that Friday night, and he did not come back until one or two o'clock Saturday afternoon. In the way the house was built, I could see him coming down the road.

We started arguing soon as he parked the car next to the house. He went inside and I went to the woodpile, got the axe, and broke out the lights. He heard the noise and he came out running. He yelled, "Luwenia, have you lost your mind?" We fussed and fought most of the afternoon. It was so much fussing going on that day, I had to call the sheriff. The sheriff warned him to stop the fighting. My husband was ashamed to leave the house with that "busted up" car. He fixed the windows with a cardboard box. The children didn't want to ride in that car with "hand-made" windows.

Wilbert did not want to involve me in his life. The only enjoyment I had was my Jesus and children. My mind was still focused on having better things in life. Those things can be accomplished if you set your mind to it. I realized that the boys were old enough to understand what I was talking about. When Wilbert was at work, I began making plans with them. I told them the first step for me was to get a job and save my money in order to get the things we need. We needed a refrigerator badly. The boys asked, "Mama, did you say you had a little bit of money?" Let's go to the store to see if you can get a refrigerator. The summer is coming and this will be our first time ever having a refrigerator. Wouldn't that be great?" I said, "Yes!"

We went to the store and looked at stoves and refrigerators that were on sale. I always wanted a brown refrigerator and stove. As we were browsing around, I saw a refrigerator and stove in a corner. I asked, "How much would I have to pay down on both of these?" I think I had about $28.00 in my pocket. I was going to get the refrigerator, if not the stove. The man acted like he knew what was in my pocket. He said, "If you have $25.00, you could get them both."

Oh my God! How glad I was to pay the $25.00 down. He said that he would deliver the appliances to the house just as soon as he could get someone to load them. When we told the other children the news, they jumped up and down. They were so glad we had ice for the first time. "Just to think we won't every run out of ice again," we said.

To pay for these things, I continued to work in the fields. I was known as the "stuck-up woman". Another name they gave me was "the hard working woman". When the people in the fields saw me coming, they called me names like "greedy gut". They just don't know how much they had hurt my feelings. I learned to ignore them, because I knew this was the only way to get the things my family needed.

This time of year, I had a choice of picking beans, or cutting cabbage. I chose to pick beans. I could make more money in picking beans. It was difficult to grasp why the female contractor disliked me. She was never in my "favor." She told some of the people that she was going to stop me from picking beans so fast. She said that I was making all the money. She came to me pretending she had something important to say. She stood far away making it hard for me to hear the conversation. While trying to understand her, time would be lost. I did not stop picking beans. A while later, one of the crew members told me of her little secret.

Most contractors were happy to have reliable and dependable hard workers. Jealousy was the only reason. When it was time to go home, she tried to talk seriously; I did not trust her. For instance, as she was taking me home, she said, "Louvenia, you beat the field today." I would say, "Oh really, that's nice."

Chapter Eight

A Struggle for Change

As I continued to work for people in 1965, I was able to save enough money to buy a television. The children were glad to get a television, because they had never seen one. When the boys were smaller, they used to go to my sister's (Beatrice) house to watch it. When they came home, they talked about "The Red Skulle Show". Phyllis thought that Red Skulle was a horror movie and not a comedy show. Clinton and Rodney watched cowboys and Indians and Robin Hood, their favorite.

When I came home from work one day, Clinton and Rodney had been playing with handmade swords. They made the swords from shaven sticks of wood. They saw people fighting with swords on television and it looked like fun. I told them once before not to play rough, because someone was going to get hurt.

What happened that day was so dangerous for Clinton and Rodney. Clinton reached out to get Rodney with the pointed wooden sword, but Rodney got him first. Rodney stuck Clinton with the stick and it broke off into his hand. A larger part of the stick was stuck into his arm. It wasn't just a splinter that broke off in my child's flesh; it was part of a stick. I could tell by Clinton's face that he was in pain. I had to do something quick. The blood circulation was blocked by the piece of wood lodged in the upper arm, thus causing a knot on the back of the hand. I did not know what to do. The first thing I did was to get a razor blade. In my heart, I knew it was not going to hurt as much the stick was, but the biggest pain was getting pass the stick. Then I said, "Lord, please let me get this stick out of this child's hand".

Secondly, I had to cut around the stick. I cut a while and I cried a while. I said to myself, I can't give up now. I took a big pin to pull the stick out. I could not put much pressure on it because I thought he might faint. I prayed a prayer, stuck the pin in the stick, and it came out. As I pulled it out, the blood gushed from the wound. I went to get some cold water; I folded a cloth, and held it on his arm for a while. I felt as if I was holding my breath for a long time. What a relief that was!

A few minutes later, it stopped bleeding. I mixed some turpentine, kerosene, and petroleum together and put it on his arm, father's remedy. I would not put alcohol on it because I knew it would burn. I put alcohol around the area, but not on the spot where the splinter or stick was. Off and on, I did this for two or three days until the soreness went away.

I noticed that the wound was infected and needed something to help it drain. The only thing we had for first aid in the house was alcohol. Using what was available, I cut a piece of salted meat and rinsed off the extra salt. I placed the meat on the sore and then I wrapped a thin piece of cloth over the whole thing. No sooner than I had put the meat on the sore, you could see the fluid draining from it. It began to heal. I said, "Thank you, Jesus".

A few months later, my husband and I fought so much until I called the sheriff. They came and gave a report telling us when to meet court. The day he was suppose to meet court, Wilbert begged me not to have him put in jail or pull time. In front of the courthouse, he promised not to hit me anymore.

We went inside the courthouse and the judge asked me did I want to press charges and I said no. I gave him another chance. He did what he said for a few days. We didn't have any fussing around the house and it felt good.

A week later, it was all over and he went right back to his same old routine. We were *struggling for change,* but Wilbert just could not accept that.

Some people wanted me to work for them. They were satisfied with my work and asked me if I would help some of their kinfolk. And I said, "Yes." When I arrived at the house and getting ready to go in, the man cried, "No, no!" His wife said, "What is the matter?" The man had problems talking, so the wife translated everything for him. I did not know what was the problem or what I had done. When the man kept shaking his head to signal no, no, he must have recognized me before I recognized him. The wife said that he does not want you to work for him.

Then I stared at his face. He looked familiar! I knew that face! This was the *same* man who hit me in the stomach years ago when I was carrying my baby. He was holding onto a walker and he could just barely move. I went back home amazed! What these people didn't know was that there is a God and he sees all things. He saw what they had done to me and he didn't like it. God said that you reap what you sow.

My husband and I went to work that Saturday, but Wilbert returned home a little earlier than I did. The children said that they wanted to watch something on television, and they decided to do all their chores first. As they sat down to watch the movie, their father drove in the yard. They were mad that their father came home early. They could tell that he was angry about something by the tone on his voice. He yelled, "Why is y'all just sittin' round here doing nuttin?"

At work as I started to clean the house, something was telling me to hurry. I was really moving around that house like a whirlwind. I finally finished all the work and they took me home. When I got out of the car, I felt strange and still did not know why. The youngest daughter ran to meet me at the door to tell what happened while I was away. She said, "Daddy was standing on you bed with *he* feet." I walked in the house and said, "He did baby?" I looked around and asked what's going on. I called, "Wayne!" All the other children came to me. They had promised each other not to tell me about the fight. The other children were upset with Carla for squealing, but they finally admitted to the truth.

They said that their father yelled at Rodney to take the ashes out of the heater in the living room. Rodney was a quiet and stubborn child. He mumbled under his breath, "I ain't gonna take those ashes out of the heater". Their father said, "What did you say, boy? Don't you be sassing me!" When Rodney was getting the bucket and shovel, their father followed him. Rodney mumbled again and his father slapped him across the mouth and made it bleed. Wayne and Clinton ran in the hall because they heard a scuffle. By the time they got there, their father had grabbed Rodney in the collar. Wayne and Clinton had to pulled their father and Rodney apart. Wayne asked Rodney, "What's the matter?" Rodney did not say anything. Then, Wayne asked their father, "Why is Rodney's mouth bleeding?" In a rage, their father said, "Who do you think you is?"

The boys and their father stumbled and scuffled from the hall through my bedroom and into the sitting room. The boys picked up their father and slammed him against the wall. Then, he was pushed down onto the couch. As they struggled back into the bedroom, the boys threw him onto my bed, they started to hit him and beat him with shoes. They let their father up and they continued to fight. As they were bouncing around on my bed, he hit at Rodney. Rodney, then, attempted to kill him with the shovel. Holding the shovel, Rodney shouted, "Let me at the bastard!" Wayne and Clinton told Rodney, "Don't do it. He is not worth going to jail for." So they let him get off the bed thinking that he had calmed down.

He stopped long to say that he was not going to have any children sassing him and beating on me. His anger was kindled again as he talked to the boys. When he did that, he began enough to grab at Rodney again. Rodney said, "I am going to kill the b—." That's when the boys pinned their father against the door and said, "Enough daddy! Enough!" They let go of their father, and he put on his shoes, wiped tears from his eyes, and left the house.

He did not like Rodney during his teen years and Rodney did not care too much for his father either. Rodney stayed to himself majority of the time and he became very quiet when his father came home. Rodney had nothing to say to him. He avoided him as much as possible, and he lost all respect for his father.

Knowing that the beginning of school was near, my children needed school clothes and supplies. To make money quickly, I went into the bean field knowing that it was that time of the month; I thought. As the day went by, I started to bleed heavily. I needed some extra protection so, I took off one of my shirts and used it for padding. This helped me to make it through the day and finally they took me home.

My condition worsen by the next morning, therefore I was unable to go to work. The hemorrhaging caused me to be so weak that I sent Phyllis to the neighbor's house to call my husband. As I sat waiting in the chair at the front door, I saw my husband come up the lane driving like a bat out of h—. Dust was flying everywhere. He drove me to the hospital. They examined me and sent me home within one day. The doctor said, "She's not going to live long, carry her back home." The doctor warned me years ago about working in the field. He also told me that my health was failing because of previous miscarriages. He told me that my body could not take anymore abuse. And another reason for the breakdown was because of the constant fighting at home with my husband. Returning home, I stayed in bed for weeks. My health did not improve.

I had been lying in bed so long and was not getting well. Waiting for the Lord to carry me home, I had given up and didn't feel like fighting anymore. The children was told to stay together just in case I was going to die. The next morning, something said to me just as plain as day. "Louvenia, get up!" Who is this telling me to get up? It said it again. "Get up!" I sat on the side of the bed and obeyed the voice. In a little while, I stood up. While standing, most of my weakness left me. A thought came to me, I believe I can walk and I did. It was a miracle! The devil tried to make me think that I was really going to die. Thank God I did not listen to him.

I had not cooked in about four weeks. I went to the woodpile and picked up some chips to start a fire in the stove. I kept saying, thank you Lord! God gave me strength to put on some beans. Since the pigtails take longer time to get done, we've cooked the beans in one pot and pigtails in the other. I made several trips outside getting chips to put in the stove while praising the Lord. The beans were finally done and they were placed on back of the stove. Meanwhile, the pigtails were still cooking. I could not believe this was a miracle!

I put some flour in a bowl, made biscuits, and put them in the oven. A bag of dried apples were also cooked. The pigtails were finally done. They were drained, and poured into the pot with the beans. After cooking the food, I went back to bed. Soon, the children got off the school bus and walked to the porch.

I went to the window and looked out to see my boys sitting down on the porch talking to each other. They were saying how glad they would be when mama gets well. She has been sick for a long time. Then, all at once Clinton said "Wayne, I smell some food." Both of them jumped up at the same time and ran into the house. The children did not know what to do when they saw me up and moving about. When they finished eating, that's when I told them what happened to me. We talked until they fell asleep at the table.

When I really got my strength back, I asked my mom to take care of my baby. Even though the doctor's told me not to work in the fields anymore, I worked anywhere to make some money. I would alternate between cleaning houses and working the field. The children needed so much! Wilbert kept all his money.

He only spent money buying one chicken for nine people on a Saturday night and I would not see him until early Sunday morning. The chicken was spoiled when I cooked on Sunday because it was left inside of his the car for hours. We very seldom got a fresh chicken or any other meat.

Sometimes he gave a little money during Christmas. Most of the time, I had to add money to buy one toy and a few clothes for each child. He bought one bag of oranges, one bag of apples, 2 or 3 bags of candy, and one turkey for nine people. Christmas time was the happiest for the children. We did not have much but it made me feel good to see them happy.

When the boys were in the 9th, 10th, and 11thgrades, their father wanted to take them out of school to work in the field. But, I would not let him. My goal was to see them graduate from high school. This was something that no one else had done in my family. With the help of the Lord, I *struggled* to keep my children in school.

One day, Wayne told me that there was a job opening. They needed someone to drive a school bus. The young man quit driving the bus and wanted Wayne to finish out the year. Since he had just got his driving license, he quickly accepted the job. He got up early the next morning and went to school. Returning home from work, the school bus was parked in the yard.

Late one night, in February of 1966, one of my brothers came to my house to tell me that my mom was in the hospital. He said that I needed to come to the hospital right away because they were not expecting her to live beyond the night. I cried as I hurried to the hospital to see her one last time. When I got there, she was having strokes one after another. I wanted to see and touch her for the last time. She died that night.

When it was time for the funeral, it was cold and rainy. As the people came in and out of the small church, birds came inside. The birds landed on my mother's coffin. I had never seen that happen before in my life. It was hard to understand but it was a sight to see.

The school year ended and my oldest son wanted to work for the summer. He said, "Mother, I am going to the beach to work for the summer. We need to get a car." The boys and I worked hard trying to save money for a new car. Later, Clinton and Rodney got a job at the Holland Inn. Their hourly wage was $4.00. The boys and I got our money together and bought a Bonneville. We paid the down payment and the car dealer gave us the keys. We came home, gathered all the children, and went for a ride. That was our first car.

All of us got ready to go to church in the Bonneville one Sunday. Wilbert said, "Nobody is going to church d'day." I said, "Yes I am going too!" Wilbert said, "Well, y'all might as well go upstairs and take off those clothes, because the girls ain't going nowhere!" I said, "You may stop the girls and you may stop the boys, but you won't stop me!" The boys said that they were going too. So the boys and I got in the car. Just as we were about to pull off, my husband ran to the car with the gun and said, "Get out, all of y'all!" Wayne said, "Daddy, you can't kill all of us at the same time. "Y'all ain't going to church, now get out!" Wilbert said. At one point, my son, Wayne, tried to persuade his daddy to not shoot the gun. As Wilbert was talking, Rodney sneaked out of the back seat of the car and ran to the back of the house. He picked up a clothesline pole, came up behind his father, and hit him on the back of the legs with the pole. He fell to the ground, Rodney got back in the car, and we drove away. As we were leaving, we saw him stumbling inside the house with the gun.

When we got back home, we didn't know what to expect. Wayne opened the door slowly and cautiously. Our eyes searched all corners of the room before we entered. He opened the door wider and we saw him sitting in the chair where he normally sits. We watched him to see if he was going to try something again, but he didn't.

Soon after this incident in 1967, Wayne was drafted into the Army during the Vietnam War. He made up his mind to enlist in the Air Force. Clinton and Rodney continued to work nights at Holland Inn. They did not keep the white car long. The power steering mechanism broke and it couldn't be fixed. Clinton bought a dark blue Chevrolet. He loved that car. Every time you see him, you'll see his girlfriend. All the kids at the high school went crazy over that car.

A year after my mom passed away, I was informed that my sister Sheila was dying. She was only 39 years old. The doctor suspected food poisoning. She asked for me to come to the hospital. As I entered the room, she motioned me to come closer. Moving slowly to her bedside, she asked for forgiveness. Theola, being in the room, overheard the conversation and asked, "Forgiveness for what?" I told her to ask Sheila. Theola said, "Louvenia, what are you talking about?" I said, "She knows. I caught her with Wilbert." Theola asked Sheila, "Did you do that to Louvenia?" She said nothing, but tears rolled down the side of her face. Sheila cried and regained enough strength to say, "I dated him a few times." Theola turned away from Sheila and wept softly. I said my good-byes and left the hospital that day feeling sad knowing that I would never see her alive again. We buried my sister a few days later.

When Carla was growing up, she was very hardheaded. When she was about five or six years old, she got a bike for Christmas. She rode the bike on the highway all the time. My nephew gave my children a German Shepherd puppy. We named him Buster. When it was a puppy, Wilbert kicked Buster hard enough to make him squeal for some unknown reason. As Buster grew, he growled every time Wilbert came near him. He just did not like Wilbert, plain and simple. Even though the older children fed and took care of him, he seemed to love Carla the most. He followed her every where.

We lived down a dirt lane, which went all the way back to the woods. The path was about a ½ mile long. That hardheaded girl rode her bike to the woods. She had no idea what danger awaited her. Carla found some way and time to get to the woods. What peaked her interest, I did not know.

The men tending the field told her to go back home before she got shot, because there were hunters nearby. The path could lead her all the way to where her father worked in the "desert" (no trees). The men had seen bears and deer in the woods while they cleared away the trees. They told her father about her being in the woods. He came home and warned her about being there. If he hears about her being in the woods again that he was going to spank her.

She didn't do that again, but she ventured into something else. She was forbidden to ride the bike on the highway. One day she took a chance riding the bike anyway. Carla started pedaling her bike fast when she saw her father coming down the road. She was trying to beat him home. He came in the house and was upset with her. He told her, "If I see you on the highway again, I am going to spank you." "Yessuh", Carla replied. Do you think that she heard what he said?

The next day, her father saw her in the road again. She did the same identical thing. She pedaled that bike so hard you could see dust coming from the wheels.

She jumped off the bike and ran into the house. Her father came in. She looked sheepishly at him waiting to see what he was going to do. He came in, looked at her, smirked, and said, "I saw you, hard-headed thing." The only thing that Wilbert did was to hit her with his cap. I thought he would at least hold up to his end of the bargain. He would have not done the rest like that!

One afternoon after school, Carla decided to ride her bike again. She was waiting for her friend that lived across the highway to come out and play. From the moment Carla got home from school, she and Buster had played outside for an hour. Maggie and Amy were babysitting.

Once Carla saw her friend outside playing, she left Buster behind. She began to pedal her bike fast and Buster was right behind her. Down the highway, a car was coming. Carla decided to cross the highway before the car reached her. She quickly pedaled across the road. When she did that, the driver started blowing his horn. Carla barely made it to the other side of the highway. The dog did not see the car, but when he finally saw the vehicle, it was too late. He ran directly in front of the car. He died instantly. The sad part was not only the dog's death; Wilbert allowed the children to see the dog lying in the ditch for several days. Since the dog disliked him, he could care less about burying Buster. A man tending the fields around us had to bury the dog. We did not have to tell Carla to stay off the road any more. She was very hurt and scared because her pet died. She seldom rode that bike after Buster's death.

In 1968, Clinton was drafted for service but enlisted in the Marines. Soon after graduation, he left to fight in the war, too! Knowing that I had two boys fighting in the Vietnam War at the same time, was a very sad period for me. It was hard to deal with, but I asked God to please give me strength.

Rodney continued to work at the Holland Inn while his brothers were serving active duty in the military. One night, Rodney came home late from work. I got up to open the door for him. After coming in the house, Rodney didn't want to go to bed. Instead, he sat on the couch with his head hanging. I asked him what was he doing. He said he was just thinking. He would never tell me why he was in such deep thought.

I think my husband stayed mad with Rodney most of the time. The very sight of each other made them uncomfortable. Rodney carried a knife around with him all the time. He took the knife out of his pocket and started cleaning his nails. He had developed a knack for flicking a pocketknife. His father came out of his bedroom, told him to turn off the lights and go to bed. Rodney totally ignored him. He said, "Did you hear me?" Rodney did not say a word. His father said, "You hard headed devil!" He didn't bother him either!

When Rodney graduated from high school in 1969, military stopped drafting young men for active duty. Rodney decided to go live with his Uncle Clinton and Aunt Della in Connecticut. Wilbert did not hit me after his scuffle with the boys. By Rodney leaving home, I was afraid the fighting would start again.

We were still "struggling" and my husband was still trifling. He did not bring any money home to buy groceries, clothing, or anything. He worked everyday on the farm. I started working for the Jennings family. Mrs. Jennings was a seamstress. I had to clean, wash, and prepare meals for her. I was glad because sometimes she gave me clothes and even some food for my family.

I came home late from work one late afternoon. Hurriedly, I put on a pot of beans and fried 2 chickens. I wanted to wait for my husband to come home to fix him some hot biscuits. While I was waiting, I started sewing on the sewing machine. Wilbert came home from work and caught me sitting at the sewing machine instead of cooking. He got mad! He said, "Luwenia, you are just like the devil. You know I am hungry when I get home from work!" He grabbed me in the collar and pulled me up from the sewing machine.

As we were tussling, the girls ran into the den because they heard a lot of noise. The girls came in with something in their hands. Phyllis had an iron poker and Maggie later joined Phyllis with a long crooked stick. Phyllis asked him, "Daddy, what are you trying to prove?" My husband said, "What do you mean? Have ya'll lost your minds?" The girls said, "No." Phyllis said, "Well you know that mama is a woman and you are beating on her. What do you think we're going to do while you are doing that to her?" That's when Amy had an anxiety attack and fell to the floor. He stopped fighting me, left the house, and returned shortly thereafter.

I previously purchased a large freezer. I felt really proud about the food being saved for the family. The lady I was working for killed a cow and asked me, "Louvenia, do you want this cow head?" I said, "Yes!" They gave me the head. I took the head home, wrapped in paper so it would not get dirty, took it to the woodpile, and split the head in half. I removed all the lean beef from the head. When I got through, there was enough meat to fill two large pans. The meat was washed, put it into plastic bags, and placed into the freezer.

When I went back to work that Monday, everybody was laughing. I asked them, "What is going on?" In previous years, people use to take the cow heads and put it in a pot of hot water to clean it. That's the way they used to do it.

They were tickle. They asked me, "Louvenia, did you cook your heads?" I said, "No". I was asked, "What did you do with it?" I said, "I cut the beef off, washed the meat, and put it in the freezer in plastic bags."

I saw them looking at each other and the laughing stopped. When I got ready to go home, they said, "Louvenia, we are not going to give you any more cow's head. We are going to clean them like you did." I said, "Oh my Lord." That was all right. I had plenty stored for the winter. They never gave me another cow's head.

Phyllis also went to Connecticut to stay with her uncle. Phyllis was there just for the summer, but Rodney decided to stay. They both worked at the same factory.

That summer, my girls and I composed a song with lyrics and music. It really sounded good and we kept it up for awhile. Then, I told my sisters to help me make a record. They were excited about the idea of making a record. We knew that we needed money to record the song. It would be recorded in New York, and we agreed to call ourselves the "Riddick Sisters".

I wanted to make this record with all my heart, but I had no money for the trip. We made a plan on how to get the money. We decided to borrow the money from a bank. My sisters wanted everyone to meet at the bank at 4 p.m. I could not be there because I knew that I would get home late from the fields. Just because I said I could not make it, one of my sisters said, "We are going to the bank to get the money and we're not going give you a darn cent." If they understood what I was going through just for us to sing together, they would not have said such a horrible thing. Even though I did not meet them at the bank, I met them at the bus station at 8 o'clock the next morning. When I got to the bus station, they did not offer me any of the money. After I purchased my bus ticket, I had 75 cents left. I saw a male friend pass the bus station; He turned around and came back to the bus station. I borrowed $35 from him.

My sisters did not talk to me during the whole trip to New York. We arrived in New York, after seven hours and stayed overnight with a cousin. When we arrived, my sisters left me in the house alone while they went shopping to buy my cousin a dress. They still would not say a word to me. While they were away, I washed the dishes. When they returned, they still had nothing to say to me. We all stayed at my cousin's house Friday night and made the record at 12 p.m. on Saturday. The people at the recording station said we did a wonderful job and wanted us to make more. I could not stay because I had to go home to my children.

The plan was to go back home soon after we made the record, but one of my brothers invited all of his sisters to his house for dinner that Saturday night. I phoned my youngest brother (Clinton) who lives in Connecticut, where Phyllis and Rodney were staying. After talking on the phone with them, I caught a bus to Connecticut and Clinton picked me up.

I talked with my two children and told them how I was treated. Phyllis asked my sister-in-law to take us shopping for clothes. My daughter bought me a dress and undergarments. When I returned, Rodney gave me $20, Phyllis gave me $40, and my sister-in-law and brother gave me $12. This made me so happy because I didn't think that my children had that much money to spare.

Clinton drove me back to New York, along with Phyllis and Rodney, for the dinner at my older brother's (Clayton) house. When I got out of the car, one of my sisters made a nasty comment. She said, "Look at her. She thinks she is something now 'cause she got on a new dress." I paid no attention to her. Angrily, Phyllis said, "That's right!"

We met both Clayton and Jerome at the door. As Clayton showed me his new home, I told him how the sisters treated me. He was very upset about the whole situation. Together, Clayton and Jerome gave me $32.

After dinner, we decided to return home in the morning. The next morning, we walked to the train station from our brother's house in Long Island. As we were walking to the train station, they said, "We ain't going to pay nobody's bus fair back home." I knew they were referring to me. I did not say a word. They didn't know that I had money. We caught the train from New York City and transferred from a train to a bus to Norfolk. When we got to Norfolk, Beatrice called her husband to come pick her up. As we were standing in the bus station, Beatrice said, "Louvenia, you and Ida are not going home with me. Y'all jus' gonna have to catch the bus to town." I said, "We've got money and we can ride to town." Beatrice's husband arrived at the bus station, but Ida and I did not get in.

Beatrice's husband asked, "Why aren't Louvenia and Ida riding with me?" The next thing he said was, "If they can't go, nobody can. So, get in the car." Beatrice told her husband to make them pay the same fare as if they were riding the bus home. He said, "If you are not paying, they aren't paying." When we got home, Ida and I stuffed the money in his pocket anyway. Beatrice wanted us to put the money in her hand, but we didn't. She got so angry that she wanted to fight.

A few hours after I got home, I noticed a taxi coming up the lane. It was Harriet! She came to borrow money from me to help pay Theola's electricity bill. I said, "I have no money for Theola." She got back in the taxi and went back home. Later that day, another taxi came up the lane. This time it was Beatrice. I could not believe all the trash she said to me, there and back on our trip. She had the nerve to show up at my door. She wanted to pay the electricity bill because she was going to spend the night at Theola's. Beatrice told me that she had no electricity in her house either. I told her, "You might as well get back in the car because I do not have any money for you or anyone else. And I mean it."

We sang together for a few years until Harriet separated from the group and moved to Connecticut to live. While Harriet was there, she started singing solo. It was not as easy as she thought. She called to ask if the sisters were going to come to Connecticut. I could not leave my children because they were too young and I wanted them to finish school.

Chapter Nine

The Last Fight

Wayne came home on leave and while he was home, he bought me a brown kitchen table, cabinet, and china. That was the first time anyone had done anything like that for me. He bought a new dark green 1970 GTO, Super Sport for himself. Wayne was teaching Phyllis how to drive a "straight" shift down the highway. He thought that she could drive well enough to drive by herself. This particular day, Phyllis was practicing driving in the yard. She drove too close to the porch and nipped it with the car. She was so upset that she jumped out of the car, left the door opened, and told Wayne what happened. He checked the car and found a small dent in the door. Phyllis ran upstairs to her bedroom to get the money to pay for the damage. He said, "Don't worry. The insurance will take care of it."

Phyllis graduated from high school in 1970 and won a scholarship to attend Beauty Academy. We, (her sisters and I) were very happy for her, but I knew that this was going to cost me extra money. The extra money paid for uniforms, rent and supplies, and her transportation. Knowing this, we worked hard to get the money she needed. Wilbert did not help out at all.

That summer I went back to New Jersey looking for summer work. I needed money. Phyllis didn't have to attend school until the fall. I left her with Maggie, Amy, and Carla. After my arrival, I went job hunting and found one the next day working at a laundry. I did not know how to do that kind of work, but I soon learned how to use the machines efficiently.

My bosses showed me how to fold clothes and how long the packages were supposed to be. There was a conveyor belt for the clothes and linen to move from one place to another. My main job was pressing large and small napkins. I was instructed to alternate; pressing the large and small napkins. One of the girls that worked there threatened to tell the boss and that he was going to fire me. She told the boss that I was taking more of the smaller napkins off the assembly line than the larger ones.

The other ladies working with me told the boss that the girl was lying. "We're standing right here watching everything and nothing like that has happened. The baskets that she is taking off are just right." Later, the boss fired her for lying. I stayed a little while longer and the Spirit told me to go home. I always put Jesus first and the children next. I came back home just in time for the girls to start school. Wayne carried Phyllis and I to Virginia to find the Beauty Academy. We rode about two hours. We finally found the school, and Phyllis enrolled on the same day.

During the fall of 1970, I kept telling the girls this was going to be the last Christmas that they were going to receive presents for a long time. I wanted to buy a house! I began working at a Rest Home. Everyday I wondered how I was going to get to work, because my husband would not take me. Some days I walked seven miles, I caught rides, or rode in a taxi.

Finally, we (children and I) were at a turning point of our lives. We were fulfilling our goals and dreams! Somehow, this felt right! Wayne and Clinton were home from the Vietnam War but they did not tell the family of their experiences when they were in service. And we never asked. Clinton served his term and moved to Connecticut in 1971 with Rodney in his apartment.

Wayne fell in love with a young lady while in service and soon after, they were married. Wayne was stationed at the Air Force Base and his wife continued to stay on campus at the university until she graduated. Rodney decided to get an apartment close to home and he needed the apartment as soon as possible. In order to get the apartment, he had to be married. Phyllis pretended to be his wife. They got the apartment without any hassle. He brought his expecting girlfriend and two children from Connecticut to the apartment.

A few weeks later, Clinton (my son) came home from Connecticut. He followed Rodney to Virginia to share the apartment. All three of them got a job at the shipyard but on different shifts. Since Wayne and his wife also needed a temporary place to stay, he moved into the same apartment, which was across the street from the shipyard. They came home occasionally during the weekends.

In the spring of 1971, Phyllis also came home on weekends. I had been in the field cutting cabbage, which was hard work. Our crew could load a trailer in 13 minutes. It turned cold that day and it started to snow. I did not wear enough clothes, so I was very cold. When we got through loading the trailer, the contractor took everyone home.

When I got home, I washed a load of clothes, hung them on the line, and started supper. I had cooked a pot of limas (butter beans). Again, I was waiting to bake the bread last and sat in the rocker behind the oil stove trying to get warm. Wilbert came in and saw me sitting in the chair. He scolded, "Luwenia, you know I always sit in that chair!" I just sat right there. Meanwhile, Wilbert turned around and went outside mumbling to himself. Phyllis said, "Mom you better get something to fight with, because daddy has gone outside for some reason!" She heard him say that he was going to kill me. I said, "Wilbert better not start 'nothing' tonight." He came back in the house with some sticks. He hit me with one of those sticks across my left wrist and blood flew everywhere. I was in so much pain. He picked up the rocker and threw it in the middle of the floor and broke it. While picking up another stick, I ran upstairs. Phyllis and Maggie followed me upstairs asking what was I going to do. I told Amy and Carla stay back.

I went upstairs to the boy's bedroom where I knew there were three gun shells in the drawer. Before I could get back downstairs, we met on the steps. Wilbert started yelling, "I am going to kill you tonight!" Taking a few steps towards me he asked, "What are you looking for, the bullets? They are not in there. I got 'em."

I grabbed the gun and jabbed it in his face knocking out two front teeth. He stumbled and fell backwards. The wall broke his fall and blood splattered. He went out of the house crying. I thought that he was looking for more sticks. But it took a long time for him to return. Phyllis helped me to change my bloody dress because my arm was hurting and swollen. While I was nervously waiting, he came back into the house covered with mud. Phyllis told me that we had to leave. As Phyllis and I were walking down the road, Wilbert stopped to ask if we wanted him to take us anywhere. I said, "No!" "Go on!" We walked to the store, which was at the end of the road. We caught a ride to Theola's house. When my sister saw my bruised and swollen arm, it made her hot! She wanted to kill Wilbert herself. After I explained to her about Wilbert, she did not care too much for him.

After *the last fight*, I stayed with Theola for a little while. I was still working at the rest home and slept home for short periods. I had a little girl that needed my attention. One morning as the children were getting ready for school, I caught a ride with my husband to work. Just before he passed his workplace, we started fussing and he got mad with me. He stopped the truck and told me to get out! I still had four more miles to go before reaching the rest home. That morning, the children's school bus rode passed me as I walked to work.

Everywhere I looked, everybody had nice homes and I had nothing. My mind was focused on buying a house that year in March 1971. The more I worked, the more I thought about my house. I was going to get one if it was the last thing I do! Finally, I was able to save some money and buy a house for myself! I just couldn't believe it!

On one of my visits to see the girls, I was cleaning Wilbert's room. I noticed two coats hanging behind his bedroom door, covered with dust and cobwebs. One coat was brown and the other was gray. I wondered why he kept those coats hanging in his bedroom. I looked in his pockets and found money, which made me mad. He always pretended not to have any money. I took enough to buy the children food and pay for my room and board at Theola's.

In June 1971, Phyllis graduated from the Beauty Academy. That summer, Maggie found a job at the Base. We both stayed at Theola's house that summer and left Amy and Carla with their father. It was hard on them staying with their father, because they were so lonely. It was the best thing I could do for them at that time. The boys came to visit sometimes. Amy and Carla had not seen me for a whole week. One Friday night, the girls tried to steal away with Clinton and Phyllis to Theola's house to see me. Amy started walking toward Clinton's car. Wilbert asked Amy, "Where are you going?" Amy said, "I am going to see my mama and you can't stop me!" Wilbert said, "Y'all ain't going nowhere!" Amy told Carla to come and get in the car. That made Wilbert mad! Clinton and Phyllis told Amy to keep her mouth close, but she kept fussing with her daddy. He was so furious that he followed them to the car. Amy and Carla were already inside when she saw her father coming. She locked the doors. Teasingly Amy said, "You can't get me now!" Clinton and Phyllis drove off.

In August, Maggie went back home to finish her last year in high school. By that time, I was working two jobs. I had a part time job as a cook at the restaurant and a full time job at the rest home. I had a plan to finish repairing the house.

Everybody was home that weekend except Phyllis. The owner of the restaurant gave me a big bag of chicken that Friday night and I forgot it. I sent Clinton and Maggie to pick up the bag the next morning. On their way back home, they were crossing the new four-lane intersection near our house. A car crashed into them and totally wrecked Wayne's car. The neighbors rushed to our house to tell us that my children were in a terrible accident. Rushing to the scene of the accident, all I could think about was, my children may be dead. As we got closer, we saw the children standing besid the car. When I saw the wrecked car, I realized that this was truly a miracle! The saddest thing to me was that my son was handcuffed and taken to jail because of his terrible driving record.

We bailed him out of jail that same night and we got a court appointed lawyer to represent Wayne and Clinton. Even though Wayne was not involved in the accident, he owned the car. Maggie, now 17, a passenger in the car, had to be a witness. The case was thrown out of court because the other driver did not show up. That was a happy moment for the family. Shame was evident as I watched Clinton's face. I hope he learned a valuable lesson that day.

I came home to see the children during the week when Wilbert was at work. When I knew it was time for him to come home, I took a taxi back to Theola's house. I continued to travel to see the children every other weekend for almost a year. Wilbert caught me home, he fussed.

Wilbert started buying food for the last three children. He bought them anything they wanted to eat. When

Wilbert asked the girls what they wanted to eat, I said, "Tell him what you want plus extra meats (chicken, baloney, etc.)." The girls were told to place the extra meats at the bottom of the freezer and the vegetables on top. We hid the can food in the bottom of the military bags and placed clothes on top. In this way, he would see only a little bit of meats and would buy more.

In the spring of 1972, Maggie wanted to go to the prom that year and I had no money. While waiting for the State Board, Phyllis was a part-time instructor and a wig stylist. Phyllis bought her a pink-laced dress with white shoes. Maggie went to the prom that year with Wayne's brother-in-law.

While working in the wig shop, Phyllis wanted her sisters to spend the day with her. Paying for the tickets, she and her sister caught a bus to Virginia and directly to her job. After work, she showed them her apartment and they all ate lunch together. At end of the day, Phyllis and her sisters rode the transit bus to the Bus Station making sure they returned safely home. By the expression on the girls' faces, I could tell they really enjoyed themselves!

Chapter Ten

A Move on My Own

Wilbert didn't like the idea of me staying to two houses. I think he wanted me to make a decision to stay with him or leave. But one of the decisions that I did make was to never sleep with him again! I had a feeling that something was about to break. And sure enough, it happened!

Wilbert told me one day, "Luwenia, you have to move because I want to bring my woman in." But, what he did not know was that I had already made a down payment on my house. Secretively, we kept taking furniture out of the house through early spring, a few pieces at a time. We dropped furniture down the road, busting up drawers from dressers, but I did not let that stop me. We continued to move furniture for several months.

One Friday evening after work, I asked a man to help me move some furniture out of the house before Wilbert came home. If there were some one else who had a truck, I surely would have asked him. This man moved like a snail! Maggie and I were moving faster and faster trying to get all the furniture out of the house. There were two beds and dressers upstairs, but time was running out. Our last trip to the truck, my husband caught us moving the furniture. He was puzzled and disturbed. The truck driver quietly went to his truck. Wilbert asked me why was I taking the furniture. I told him that I bought a house in the city. After I told him about my house, he changed his mind about the other woman.

Nobody was saying a word. He started crying and making plans for us to be together in my new house. He said, "Oh, I see." I'll stay here until Clinton's car is moved and them I come later." I told him it was too late. Wilbert said, "Luwenia we both have said some things that we did not mean." Maggie and I got in the truck with the driver and we drove away. Wilbert was still standing in the yard when I left. After 28 years, of abuse, it was finally over, no more fighting! Thank God!"

As we rushed back to town to unload, Maggie was preparing to graduate the next day, June 1972. Maggie, Amy, Carla, and I moved to Theola's house. School was closed for the summer break. While I was waiting for my new house to be fixed, I left a few things at the old house. I knew that I had to move somewhere because Theola was a pain.

In July 1972, the four girls and I were walking down the street with buckets of water and mops to repair and clean my new house on Sundays, which were my days off. The house was located on the next street from the rest home. After work, I did a lot of repairs to the house myself, because the house had been originally condemned by the city. In order for me to live in the house, it had to pass inspection. The Housing Inspector gave me a list of repairs. Some of the requirements were to have running water, rewiring, plumbing, and the back porch must be repaired. The inspector only gave me thirty days to complete all these repairs according to the standards.

Theola's house was on the other side of town from my house, which was a great distance to walk. We were on our way to clean the house when a white man asked us if we needed a ride. I said yes and we all piled in the car. As we were riding in the car, the water sloshed around in the buckets. We kept eyeing each other afraid that the water was going to spill on the car floor. When we got there, the man looked at the house and then he looked at us. I was ashamed and the reason was obvious.

It was an unpainted three-story house. In the backyard, there were two very, very large pecan trees and a small one. No one lived in the house for a number of years and the leaves had begun to pile up. The house had visible damaged beams and a large tree limb had fallen through the front porch roof. The back and front porches had rotten boards. On the second floor, pigeons made nests on the eaves, and the squirrels made nests in the walls of the third floor. Through all of this, I was not going to give up. I needed my house and I was going to do all I could to get it done! I hired a carpenter to fix the front porch roof and the back porch.

When the inspector returned, he tested the porch floor by jumping up and down on the new boards. The man cursed because the boards were so firm and neatly put together. He really did not expect the house to pass inspection. Thank God he passed it anyway. When he did that, I was so happy! We continued to repair my house; it was hard work.

I had to pull up old planks, old linoleum, old wet carpet, plastered walls, and old curtains. We threw all of it outside in the backyard. When I say trash, I am talking about leaves and trash piled up almost to the second floor balcony. We cleaned all the junk out of the house and we did not stop until we got it finished. My sons did very little to help with the repairs because they had jobs and families of their own.

While I was waiting for the people to rewire my house, I paid Theola, rent for all the girls and me. The oldest daughter would come home on the weekends.

Maggie had begun to date a young man. Theola had a picnic table and benches outside in the yard. The boy came over to see my daughter and they sat on the table talking and doing what a teenage couple would do. My oldest sister, Ida, spied on them from an upstairs window with the lights off. She said they were making love on the table, which was not true.

She told my daughters that they were no good and that your mama was no good, either. The girls got very angry and told her that she had a nerve sleeping with a married man, with only a thin curtain separating our bedrooms. Theola was trying to get Ida to be quiet but she got worst. Ida was so mad that she was ready to fight the girls. Even though the girls told me about the argument, we still were not ready to move into our house. I told my girls to be patient a little while longer and not to worry about their aunts. I said, "We will not in Theola's house much longer."

We worked all through the summer and into late August. It was time for the girls to go back to school. Maggie walked to a nearby college and the other two went to public schools. There were two schools in the neighborhood and I didn't know which one Carla was suppose to attend. The only thing I knew to do was to send her to Phillips Elementary School, a school in the area. After four days, I assumed everything was going well. I was totally wrong! Procedures, rules, and regulations had changed. I was not aware of the changes. Things were so different now than when I attended school. I lost touch with reality trying to make a living for my children and I.

I later learned that the principal demanded the secretary to take Carla to the auditorium. She asked the secretary what had she done wrong. The secretary said nothing but ordered Carla to sit in the auditorium by herself for one hour. They took so long, she decided to go to the office. They sent her back into the auditorium. At this point, Carla began to cry. In the mornings, Carla caught rides with one of the teachers and secretary, occasionally. She overheard the principal threatening the teacher and the secretary. He told them not to bring her to school anymore or they would lose their jobs.

Finally, the secretary asked her to come in, the principal walked up to her, and he began to scold at my daughter. He said, "Get out my school and if I catch you in this school again, I'm calling the police to have you escorted off the property! You are in the wrong school district!"

Only ten years old, my daughter walked from the school to Beetle's Lane approximately 10 o'clock in the morning, which is about a mile, crying. The office called me after my daughter got home. I did not know what to do. The next day, I decided to enroll her to another school, P. C. Shannon, down the street from my sister's house. They said that she was too old. The grade level only went to the third grade. She was promoted to the fourth grade. We walked to another school and it was B. T. Branch. Carla attended that school for a short while.

I had to enroll Carla to another school, S. L. Ram, after another big argument between Ida and me. This house also had no running water and no electricity! You know, I wondered when was I ever going to have the good things in life. The only thing different about this house was that it was mine! The house had to be inspected one more time.

We had everything completed except electricity and running water. The inspector extended the time for us to complete the work while we lived in the house. We needed water, so I asked my father to drill a hole in the ground for an outdoor pump, until the pipes were repaired.

The girls and I worked hard all day in the house. We each chose our favorite bedrooms. The curtains were hung, walls were painted, rooms were decorated, and the beds were made. It was beginning to look like a home. Or should I say, my HOME! This was the beginning of a new life for me and it felt good! *A Move on My Own*!

Luella Thomas

About the Author

Born on August 1, 1927 in a rural township in the Eastern part of North Carolina, Luella R. Thomas was the fifth child of thirteen children. Lacking the education and wealth to succeed, she worked diligently as a housekeeper and a laborer for much of her life. Knowledge was obtained from everyday experiences and challenges that no formal institution could provide. Life was a good teacher.

The greatest teacher, of course, was the church. Gospel music and songs offered spiritual relief from some of her troubles. She felt compelled to jot down a few lines on anything she could find, even cardboard boxes, to express some of her most horrible nightmares.

As years passed, she became a caregiver for the mentally challenged, homeless, and the elderly including her father. She is now highly regarded as a zealous advocate of truth and integrity by her family, the church and the community. Luella is also the matriarch of the Thomas clan with her seven children being the first benefactors of her loving influences.